CONSCIOUSNESS

IS LIFE

Darwin Gross

CONSCIOUSNESS IS LIFE

ISBN: 0-931689-04-X

Library of Congress Catalog Card Number: 82-081647

Typed on MacIntosh by Jean Strong
Edited by Bernadine Burlin
Typeset on Apple Lazer Writer

Printed in the U.S.A.

SOS Publishing
P.O. Box 68290
Oak Grove, Oregon 97268

"If man's concept of himself and the world around him was different, everything in this world would be different. His concept of himself being what it is, everything in this world must be as it is. As you can see, it is up to you, the individual, to change your consciousness through the spiritual exercises of the Ancient Masters which can assist you, and by actually changing your concept of yourself, you can build upon your daydreams. In this way, you can experience the results of these concepts in your world, here and now!"

"Cause-Substance: Your Consciousness"
Darwin Gross, January 1979

INTRODUCTION

The Ancient Masters and their science leads to an understanding of what consciousness is. Those that follow them in consciousness learn from them, as have enlightened individuals throughout the ages, that it is man's state of consciousness which determines the conditions of his life. Through techniques given in the study of the teachings, the serious student can develop himself spiritually to move from the human state of consciousness to a God-realized state while still retaining a balanced, normal day-to-day life.

Life is a continuous, consecutive series of opportunities to be taken advantage of or lost. Spirit is that essence which emanates from the creative center called God in the universes, in the higher levels of existence. This essence or force radiates through all existence levels down to the lowest, permeating all things. It flows through every individual, and, whether consciously or unconsciously, that person's mental attitudes, thoughts and emotions shape the way it is manifesting in his life. One comes to realize that we can become conscious focal centers or distribution centers for the positive spiritual force that can work through us as vehicles.

If one wants to achieve spiritual unfoldment or spiritual evolution, it requires a certain amount of effort. Your spiritual evolution will be determined by your understanding of what you must give for it and what you will receive from it. No person on the path of life is forced to become anything that he does not want to be, because this would be a violation of spiritual law. If

you wish to become a spiritual giant, you must first
realize you have the potential to become that.

It reminds me of an experience I had some time ago
after work at night. Occasionally I run around a
quarter-of-a-mile track near a high school, and I hadn't
been doing this too long, but I thought to keep the
physical vehicle from getting too rusty that it might be
good to work it just a little bit. So I was out on this track
one night and I saw an older man running around, and
he had a very smooth gait; it was almost like water
flowing the way he moved around that track. He was
probably in his early sixties. Full of confidence, I
moved up behind him about 25 feet and proceeded to
follow him around the track, sure that I could keep pace
with him. After the first half mile at the pace he was
going, I was exhausted. I stopped, took a breather,
while he continued to lope around again. I got back in
the track behind him because I didn't want to suffer any
embarrassment by risking a position in front of him
where he could pass me, and another quarter mile
went by. I thought after my breather I certainly should
be able to keep up with this fellow; and I got tired again
and after a mile I just quit in disgust, while this man
continued to go by.

It illustrated to me that in this particular event or
activity, this man was superior to me. He obviously had
run around that track more often than I had, had
invested more effort in the mastery of this activity than
I. Yet I knew that with determined practice I could get to
the same level he was at. I had that potential within me.

The same is true, in a sense, of the spiritual life.
There is a difference between a master, the teacher,

and the student. The Master has gone around that track before you many times. You cannot keep pace with the master until you have achieved master status yourself. You have the potential to do the same and accomplish as much as the spiritual traveler, but you must also realize that you have that potential and you have to make the effort.

There have been masters on Earth throughout history whose sole job it was to help individuals uncover the potential of the God-realized consciousness within themselves. Though written referrals to the teachings of the ancient masters exist in many of man's religious scriptures, the oldest dating back as far as the Naacal records, reputed to be over 20,000 years old, the teachings were mostly passed on orally from master to student. It was Paul Twitchell, the Master from 1965 to1971, who introduced this ancient teaching to our modern society through extensive lecture tours, taped talks, study discourses, and several dozen published books, some of which are The Far Country, The Spiritual Notebook, Dialogues With The Master, The Tiger's Fang, and others. His book known as The Tiger's Fang is a description of a spiritual journey that Paul took, due to his level of consciousness, as he moved out of his physical body up through the various levels of universes beyond time and space, to eventually experience the God-conscious state and return to tell the world about it.

His successor as the Master, Darwin Gross, is continuing the work that was given to Paul Twitchell. Through public lectures, music and presenting the teachings without trying to sway the listener through emotionalism, fear or guilt, communicate via the written word, as well as work with individuals on the inner dimension.

The Master is a vehicle for what is known as a channel for the Mahanta consciousness. It is the greatest state of consciousness which goes beyond the God state. This may seem like a rather adventurous statement to make, but I know most students who have been on the path for some time and have had experience on the inner planes with the Master can verify that this is true. The Master will help you if you are under his spiritual guidance and spiritual protection, with writing, should he choose, or conversation, in your physical approach to spirituality. He also has unlimited ability to work with you on this dimension and in other dimensions internally. It always is your choice in the end to make a decison.

The state that is known as total consciousness means that this spirit consciousness can be anywhere at anytime, without drugs. It takes patience and plenty of self-discipline. If you have constructive thoughts, your consciousness will be uplifted. Positive entities will be attracted to you and positive situations also. If you engage in negative thinking you will close down your consciousness. You will make yourself a prisoner.

The story comes to mind that I heard when I was a boy, about a group of prisoners in a cell block. There was only one window in this cell block, and it was rather high, so the one convict who had a bed near this window was able, just by stepping on his tiptoes, to peer out over the window sill and see what was outside. None of the others of the group in this particular cell had the advantage of being able to look outside this window.

Every morning they would ask this friend what he would see. They were in confinement and it brightened their day, so they were all anxious to know what was going on, on the outside. So every morning very dutifully this fellow inmate would report the color of the leaves on the trees and the type of sunset or sunrise, conditions on the outside, descriptions of people passing by, and so forth.

Eventually, however, the other members got restless. Why is he the only one that is privileged to be able to look out of the window? Why should only he be the one to see all these things? So they conspired to kill him so that some other member would have a chance to get his bed and look out the window as he did, which they did do.

Another member took his bed, and when he first looked out the window the next morning they all eagerly asked him what he saw. He reared back in amazement. "I don't understand it. There's only another brick wall. I can't see anything!"

Most of us have brick walls that we build around our own perspective and our own consciousness. We cannot see. We are limited, and we limit ourselves. Spiritually a master has been beyond that wall. He can see beyond that wall. You have the choice of following someone who has moved through these worlds and can protect you and guide you so that you can do this yourself, or you can let it pass by. The choice is yours.

Dr. Paul Schoolcraft

TABLE OF CONTENTS

CONSCIOUSNESS IS LIFE
By Darwin Gross

"Remember, until you understand that nothing can happen to you, nothing can ever come to you or be kept away from you except in accordance with the state of your consciousness, you do not have the key to life." Chapter 6.

Darwin shares with us the wisdom gained on the road to mastership of the great divine spiritual current known as Spirit, to help guide you on your own journey.

"To know one's self, as Socrates put it a few thousand years ago, is really the first commandment of the Ancient Masters. It is a great opportunity to make further discoveries in the universe and the heavenly worlds, for latent in man's brain is a capacity one million times greater than he is using now. Science has perceived that the average man of today uses only a small percentage of his brain cells.

"Knowledge is never concealed from the eyes of the masses, but the masses refuse to see, note, and understand the knowledge that is right before their noses. They get caught up in emotionalism, swept into the tidal waves of astral impulses under the guise of 'good versus evil' and end up with someone else's considerations, not their own.

"Thoughts of pain and grief are the creators of what man calls old age. Through the teachings of the Ancient Masters, one learns that thoughts of love, joyfulness and cheerfulness bring about the beauty of youth. Age in the outer shell is not the gem of the true reality which lies within; the real fountain of youth is in Soul.

"The individuals who have a long list of reasons why something won't work rarely believe that their problems stem from within themselves.

" They will blame someone else, and may never learn that only when they change their attitude towards themselves and others around them, will a greater light enter their lives.

"When the pain is great enough and the burdens heavy enough, the individual often cries out in anguish: 'All right God, I give up! I surrender!' And with that inner and outer self-surrender, help is given."

Chapter 1

SLEEP UPON A DREAM

Your dreams are an important part of your life, a rebalancing of life forces and minerals within your body as well as the various spiritual bodies. As you lay your head down to rest at night, or just take a catnap in the afternoon, most of us drift off to one of the lower levels of heaven. You have a choice to do what you wish during this time period. One can learn to play some musical instrument, paint, write creatively, etc., while others may visit the museum on the astral plane, such as inventors have in the past and still do in the present, the place of the past and the future.

Those that die here on Earth and have not unfolded spiritually beyond the first two levels of heaven, wind up there and find that they must work or learn something creatively which interests them just as they do here on Earth.

There is a part of an individual's life which can be worked out in the dream state, for this area of existence to many is every bit as real (often more so) than being in the physical realm of existence. Some people have the experience where they cannot separate their day-to-day life from their dream experiences, and it can often be confusing and upsetting if they are made to feel something is wrong with them.

1

While the physical body rests, experiences occur for the sleeping individual on several inner planes. These are usually the lower levels of heaven, the astral plane and sometimes the mental plane, rarely the soul plane.

Most people have not developed the awareness of knowing where they are going when they are dreaming, yet others recall vividly their dream experiences. Some write them down so they can better understand the messages that are coming through to them from their inner lives, which deals with you only on that level. Since much of the dream state can be involved with symbols, these are usually best understood by the individual having the dream than from someone outside who does not understand where the individual is working spiritually.

The dream mechanism often utilizes a method of mind activity that differs from the awakened state of consciousness. This can be established in colors, however, most people dream in black and white, while others have two-color dreams, such as red and black. Some will take the whole spectrum of colors in their dreams.

Dreams have always fascinated mankind. Ancient kings lived and ruled according to the interpretations of their dreams, and many a dream interpreter lost his head if the interpretation did not please the king. Even the old testament is based on the dreams of the elders that were handed down years later, however changed by man many times since.

Don Horine had an article in the National Enquirer, a magazine published in the United States, saying that "the world's best-known inventions originated in the

minds of their creators while they were sound asleep."
He went on to tell how Elias Howe spent "futile years
trying to perfect the sewing machine before the
solution to his biggest problem--how to make the
needle work--came to him in a dream." When savages
were about to kill him in the dream sequence, he
noticed "small eye-shaped holes at the tips" of their
spears, which provided him with the idea that has
proven to be the answer. In the same article, Horine
told of James Watt's efforts to improve upon scatter
shots for guns which was costly to make since each
pellet had to be cast separately. "One night Watt
dreamed that he was out walking in a rainstorm and,
instead of uniting into puddles of water, the raindrops
hit the ground and remained there in pellet form." Watt
melted lead and dumped it "onto the street from a
tower" and found the street covered with tiny lead
pellets. Again, the answer came in the dream state.

Since all life is a spiritual experience, what you may
ask, do dreams have to do with one's spiritual life? And
if you are not especially interested in a spiritual life,
what does all this have to do with you?

Your life carries with it a plan that arises from past lives
you've lived before, and from what you have agreed to
prior to your entry into this present physical life
existence. Now, you don't have to believe this, yet
there are millions who know this to be true. And when
you know--you know! Much is in our libraries, referring
to birth after birth, by many authors.

Some dreams may be either veiled or vivid recall of
past lives; most revolve around one's personal and
emotional situations that surface during sleep in an

3

effort to work out problems or to cover their reality in one's life. If a financial problem exists in the daytime, it is most likely it will appear as such in the dream state. If one's health is poor, his dreams may symbolically characterize this in an exaggerated manner, since dreams tend to do this--they exaggerate in the size, shape and problem-at-hand.

Morals creep into the dream state in many ways--sexual fantasies, marriages to faceless images, attacks by often faceless aggressors, scares by wild animals. Nightmares are usually an attempt by the dreamer to extricate himself from a physical or psychic situation that he is unable to cope with when in the waking state. But they are creations he has created himself.

Once one has created the conditions that make up one's life on any and all levels of existence, he is stuck with the consequences unless he realizes what he is doing and moves to correct it.

I get thousands of letters from individuals who cry and beseech someone to take their troubles, their aches and pains, and their problems away from them.

The Dream Master can show them in the dream state how to remove these situations from their lives, but they have to do it themselves; no one can do it for them.

When the pain is great enough and the burdens heavy enough, the individual often cries out in anguish. "All right God, I give up! I surrender!" And at that inner chamber within your self you turn loose of the mental thoughts and surrender to the inner master, help is given. It may happen in the dream state or during a coincidental meeting with someone who offers a solution, or from reading a book that just might be found on a park bench or on a counter top. Some will suddenly be aware of a white light or a blue star in their inner vision, or the face of a man you just are unable to forget; it's in the gentle eyes.

It may be a spiritual guide from their own religious path, or it may be one of the spiritual travelers. When they are fortunate enough to be guided by the Master, they are taught in the dream state and taken to the Golden Wisdom Temples where they attend classes and receive assistance on their spiritual journey to the Godhead.

The Ancient Masters have been around since the beginning of time as we know time. They work on all the levels of heaven in the universes of God, and they work hand in hand with the Living Master who has been given the responsibility for a period of time on this planet and all the realms of existence.

When he steps aside as the Living Master, he is replaced with another. The worlds are never without a Living Master, although he may not be world-known as many have been, as pointed out in the works of Paul Twitchell. The Masters and most seeking the higher truths, live on such a higher level of understanding, so in tune with spirit that they are able to operate on a high work level, for as much as up to twenty hours a day and not be fatigued.

Three to four hours of sleep is all I average. The Masters live a full life, yet work on a relaxed level. We do not carry the burdens of mental strain for it is cast off into the stream of spirit. The only time it is a burden is when the Master goes out into crowds or moves about in public.

On October 22, 1971, I accepted the responsibility as the Master of the times, following the translation (death) of the previous Master, Paul Twitchell, known spiritually as Peddar Zaskq. Paul held this responsibility from October 22, 1965 until his death, September 17, 1971. There is an unbroken line of Mastership beginning with the first Ancient Spiritual Master, Gakko.

When the individual wishes to work with the Master in the dream state, he is visited nightly by the Dream Master who assists him in working out his problems, health concerns and daily situations that govern his life.

One lady wrote me that it was easier to communicate with me in the dream state than on paper or in person. This is true. When individuals are relaxed and fast asleep, they are more amenable to guidance for their spiritual unfoldment. This in turns allows the outer conflicts to dissipate. However, since they have created their world, they must work to un-create that which they don't want in their world any longer. This is often accomplished in the dream state.

If one wishes to dominate another, or their community, or the world, they in turn will find their lives dominated in a similar way. Perhaps not in this particular life, but in the next. If one has harmed another in a past life, that debt will require payment at some time or other. The ledger sheet is carefully kept with debits and credits for each and every soul that is created by the Supreme Being, which is known as Sugmad, an ancient Chinese name for God.

All of man's scriptures say in some form or another: "Ye reap what ye sow." And this accounts for the handicapped individuals or those who have such a hard life even though they seem like such beautiful people. If they cheerfully work out their handicap, whatever it may be, their future existences will be much easier to handle.

There is no God of wrath as some state, only a law of cause and effect that says for every cause man brings into being, there must be a re-action or an effect from it. Once this all-important spiritual law is understood, man uses care in his thoughts and deeds for he knows they will one day return to taunt or haunt him. The more spiritual the individual or country is, the swifter the law comes into effect.

The Ancient Teachings of the Masters are not here to change the world. It is an individual teaching with the Master as the spiritual guide and wayshower. The world and universe I'm speaking of, is your world, within yourself, and these worlds that are invisible to most eyes, physically or spiritually. It is a magnetic field, just like the ring around the moon or the Earth. These are your fields and they are yours to direct, but you must be receptive to the inner direction that guides the individual and the whole; it has been called the wee small voice.

If you are interested in science, you might be taken in the dream state by the Dream Master to the museum on the astral plane, a source of new ideas that will aid and benefit the good of all. Some learn to paint or draw or work with music while in the dream state.

That's why one should never be afraid of or put off about new skills. You can do anything you put your mind to.

There are four basic types of dreams. The sensual type of dream that is emphasized in Freud's work. It has little to do with sex as many feel it does. However, it is the pleasurable dream experience connected mainly with anything that gives pleasure to the body, such as eating and drinking.

This is one way the Masters are able to help another person with their problem, such as drinking. It is stopped in the physical yet the individual will drink in the lower levels of heaven to satisfy the need.

A second type is soul projection and is taught in the mystery schools. The Masters take the interested individual to a Golden Wisdom Temple in the dream state to study and to eventually get enough knowledge to be on his own.

Another form of dream is the memory type. It deals with the past years and lives of the memory area. It can show us how the karma affects us in our life now and can show us why we are here this lifetime.

To experience this, make a postulate that you will dream a certain part of your life in some period on the time track. Likely you may have the dream.

The fourth area of our dreams is in the spiritual realm, dealing with out of body travel, clairvoyance and precognition. One is able to step out on the time track to look at the future and learn to prophesy for one's self.

The bold and adventuresome explore the worlds of the dream state and are always under the watchful eye of a spiritual traveler, sometimes also known as a guardian angel, who sees that the individuals are protected and kept out of danger.

Those who are taken to the Golden Wisdom Temples are taught by masters in the dream state. They eventually read from the books called the The Way of the Eternal in the various Golden Wisdom Temples, learning more of the spiritual knowledge that assists them in their day-to-day existence on Earth.

The books on dreams have aided many people with its helpful guidelines to one's daily life and dream life, as well as their spiritual unfoldment. Most have read about or had interest in dreams, with some dreaming in color, some in black and white, some not recalling dreams at all.

Just as in other areas of spiritual unfoldment, the screen might be pulled, but eventually with inner guidance and direction, one can come into direct knowingness.

It can be very frightening to anyone when he is alone beyond space and time, and the fact that only he alone can agree on his individual environment.

The phenomenon of life is found within the state of consciousness of every individual. His perceptions are not bound by feeling, hearing, sight and touch. Spiritual enlightenment must be given broadness and depth of understanding for it is a two-edged sword. Only the individual within himself can find peace while he is here on this level of experience. Yet he tends to want everything done for him.

Dreams are not a cure-all, but problem-solving is best done in the dream state. The basic problem of all man's existence here on Earth is a desire for love and acceptance. The subconscious self requires social contact, creates social problems and arouses emotions in the outer mind through dreams and fantasies.

Tempers and frustrations are often the product of this subconscious mind, also known as the unconscious mind. In most cases, their origin lies in past lives from emotional problems. But these individuals can receive help from the dream master in working out their problems in the dream state. The problems are worked off, stripped away, while the sleeper is taken to the astral and mental realms.

Thinking about one's problems will not dissolve them. Instead it keeps them pinpointed in the individual's awareness. Even when a dream appears to be meaningless, if one keeps a diary of his dreams, understanding may come at a later date. With action and reaction working to keep the mind balanced, through the spiritual guide the dreamer can plan his future through dreams and find answers to his daily problems.

Certain foods can create disturbances for the dreamer, especially if eaten late at night. In time one can learn to alter unpleasant dream experiences as they occur without having to escape them by awakening.

As stated earlier, during the sleep period there is a rebalancing of one's chemicals, life-forces and a general readjustment, not of the physical body alone but of the various bodies of man.

If one is afraid to sleep because of nightmares or "bad dreams," he can build pleasant figures into his thoughts prior to going to sleep, drawing upon those he feels he can trust, acting with the belief that his nightmares are of his own creative mind and thought. If he created them, then he can un-create them. Like the artist with a pen or pencil, he can just erase whatever looms up in his dreams or challenge them, and then they will dissipate.

Should the dream state be misused against another person, the law of cause and effect will come into play immediately. Whatever the originator sends out to another will return eventually to him, good or bad. It is an impersonal and utterly relentless law, not only in the dream state, but in the psychic and physical realms as well.

Children who scream during the night may be fighting the efforts of their spiritual guide to return them to their physical bodies. This was discussed in my book, "You Can't Turn Back."

I would awaken from dreams screaming and crying, unable to tell my concerned parents about the experiences I had in the dream state. Dreams became the true reality to me and I couldn't explain the beauty and bliss I found in these inner worlds. I didn't want to return to the physical existence and had to be forced back into the body by my spiritual guide. Thus I resisted and came back to the physical realm in a state reminiscent of a nightmare.

This was very distressing to my parents who couldn't fathom their son's problem. If the child screams and cries during sleep, it isn't because of a nightmare. Soul does not want to return to the human state of consciousness, and it took my spiritual guide to assist in getting me back. Since I was only three or so at the time, my parents were about ready to give up on me over this.

I was inwardly going beyond the universe, the stars and planets in the galaxies, traveling from universe to universe and preferring the heavenly worlds because of the total freedom I experienced there with my spiritual guide, who was Paul Twitchell, although I didn't realize it then at that tender age.

Children are very open and receptive to their spiritual guides and are known to respond to them in the physical, even though those around them cannot see these invisible friends.

Paul came to me when I was very small, appearing before me in my bedroom. Our communication was silent between us, but from that moment of his appearance before me, I never knew any fear of going beyond myself into the inner worlds, which were and are very real, and the objective worlds as well.

When parents understand such incidents with their children, they can usually relax and not be worried about it. It may help to let the child know you understand what is happening to them.

Certainly an adult should never ridicule the child or put them down, for in the earlier years of their lives, children are very close to Spirit. It is as their outer selves get older that they may close off this relationship, if they are made to feel they are unusual or different from others. It turns some into introverts.

I used to daydream as a child, and while it should not be carried to excess, daydreaming has its place. It can be considered a "mini-vacation," as a refreshing and relaxing change of pace for the individual whose day is filled with frustrations and decision-making. However, one must use common sense when daydreaming, for it cost me a job once. Haven't all of the inventors daydreamed at one time or another?

The Master Lai Tsi who dwells and teaches on the etheric plane, was quoted as saying: "When one is in the awakened state of the physical senses, he is asleep. But when in the sleep state and dreaming he is alive. In other words, we only live when dreaming and long for this state when in the physical senses."

With understanding of himself, man can create a happier and more fulfilled life for himself. Sometimes we let others initiate and set up the experiences we are going to have in the dream state. How do we correct this for ourselves in our daily life, whether it is at work, at play, in some situation at home or with the people we come in contact with from day to day?

The initiate on the path learns how to guide and direct his own world and universe without letting others set up these conditions for him. With this in mind, you must realize that each thought you think must be for that moment of time, not looking to the future, but relating to the daily moments. If you have a conflict coming up and you suspect that person is going to object to what you want to do, whether it is a day or a week in advance, this can be worked out while your physical body is resting at night.

It isn't easy to turn loose of the inner desires or that which you would like to have happen in your daily life. But you can initiate it within yourself if you can turn it over to the inner master and let go of it, allowing spirit to work it out for you.

You are trying to handle what is happening in your own life, not someone else's. Too many are trying to tell us individually what we are to do with our lives--the media, newspapers, television, radio, friends, relatives, the cults and even the governments. They are trying to change your life and everyone else's life to fit their way.

Religious orders do that with their world wide programs on radio and TV, impressing guilt and fear upon their listeners, saying Jesus died to save them and you and the world from sin and bad health. This is a very negative trap, for Jesus never even wanted to be worshipped.

What really grabs my short hair is the religious push in politics in the attempt to make everyone and this nation a Christian nation, begging for dollars on the air, no better then the cults.

Man, with his religious teachings down through time, has never really tried to follow in the footsteps of Jesus, Buddha, or Mohammed, on Earth. The priestcraft have withheld much of the spiritual teachings of God from the masses.

This is nothing new to you, I am sure. Few if any followers of the church have been able to do the things the past teachers, saviors or saints have accomplished, such as: Padre Pio, a stigmatist who was adept at out of body travel and who was seen and heard in many places, hundreds of miles away from the monastery he lived in; St. Francis Xavier, the Sixteenth Century Spanish Jesuit saint, who was responsible for bringing Christianity to the Far East; St. Anthony of Padua, and St. Francis of Assisi; Pythagoras and

14

Zoroaster, St. Paul, the Apostle, Apollonius of Tyana, and a Saxon monk named Godric who witnessed Thomas a' Becket's death from a great distance--but a few of those who knew how to separate soul from the body to serve mankind.

Why is it that man is content to crawl, yet is obligated to do so? As the good books around the world state--and I'm speaking of the Christian Bible, the Koran, the Talmud of the Jews, the scriptures for the Buddhists and Sikhs, and Hindus, and such--man has been given dominion over all things. He too, was certainly given the knowledge of how to fly as the birds, in soul. One has the opportunity to learn to do this as well as to go beyond his mental means, for the fault has been in the mind of man with his teachings and his own mortal concept of himself. You must learn how to go to the temple within in order to understand more than that which is written in books.

In man's own consciousness he is limited and yet unlimited, as free or bound as he thinks and as he sees himself. Neither race nor color enter into the picture. What is good for one in spirit is also good for the next guy.

What does enter into the picture is the karmatic situation for a particular given race. Should a man who carries a load of supplies across a river or stream to save himself the inconvenience of going down the river two or three miles, be in any way a more special person than you are? If he should walk across that river with the same load--no. He or she is not created different in any way. Their atom structure would not have any more power within themselves than anyone

15

else that is created here on Earth. Everyone has the right to use the thought forces and develop the God-given powers of spirit, its use and the results.

If you want to get involved in your community, the governmental situations, politics, etc., the world you live in, that is your responsibility. It has nothing to do with one's spiritual path. We can only do so much and those who have family responsibilities must put their values in proper priority.

Keep in mind that in the pure positive God worlds there is no "form" as we know form beyond the soul level. In those endless worlds and invisible worlds, once one passes through the soul plane, it is a lonely journey on into the God-conscious plane to experience IT.

It takes an enormous amount of will power and initiative on the part of the individual to work toward the experience of not having to return to this physical realm again when one passes across the borders of heaven.

You can have the understanding of what lies beyond this physical realm and not have to wait until death to see and know of it. One can unfold into direct knowingness or cognition of what is taking place. In that state, words aren't needed, and you do not question. I'm not saying you shouldn't question until you reach that point, for doubts are healthy. I myself had to be shown; I had doubts.

Wherever you are and whoever you are, you are observed from moment to moment and even as to how you handle a certain thought in action. In time an individual becomes aware of this.

We sometimes tend to get involved in environmental changes, but spirit usually has the last word, in a sense. Being a vehicle and a co-worker for IT, which I refer to as God or Sugmad, without directing spirit in any sense of the word, you become aware as you open up to spirit that things change in your area, your city, the nation, the world. And we may have to keep quiet about some things when certain knowledge is available to us, for very few people would believe it if you told them something was going to happen if this or that were done.

The awakenings occur in time, as this young lady wrote me in the summer of 1977:

"This morning, very early I wrote down the memories of a dream I had last night. The dream wasn't particularly significant by itself, but the important thing is that it is the first time I have ever been able to discipline myself to wake up and write down a dream. I am so excited about it. It is just a few scratchy sentences but it's a first! I had asked for assistance on the inner to do this before going to bed last night and it worked, as always. I have recently begun the discourses and tomorrow is the first class, and now I can report progress. I have never experienced any difficulty with having inner experiences. This occurred quite naturally soon after I entered the study, but I do not have very clear dream recall. Lately I have had more success with this and then finally I've reached the place that I can wake up and write it down. Paul Twitchell says in his writings that after a period of months you will be able to see a trend in your dreams and a pattern will emerge. I am looking forward to this new awareness and will report on it."

Having faith in the inner master or in spirit itself, knowing that all heaven and Earth can fall away, and you are still taken care of, then you can go anywhere and be yourself amongst any type of people of any nation, knowing that the presence of that which is flowing through the radiant body of the master is from the one source that sustains all life.

This is something that you carry around with you, regardless of who you are and where you are from. It is thought of as love in these lower worlds, but the love that we think of is limited. When you reach that God-conscious state, you learn the truth of both sides of IT, or of God.

Paul Twitchell spoke of these journeys to God in his book, The Tiger's Fang. It is stressed in the teachings of the masters to go to that temple within to worship, if you wish to worship. You can visit the inner planes during a twenty-five minute contemplation, or at night in the dream state.

You may not physically, in the human state of consciousness, realize what is happening or where you have gone, but let the mind know that you are in the hands of the masters and that you are a vehicle for IT, and that is all that is necessary.

Chapter 2

THE SENSE OF BELONGING

We as human beings, man and woman, hunger for
and have the need to "belong" to another human
being, or a social community, a political cause, a
religious path, or some field that allows him or her a
feeling of security and acceptance--of belonging. This
is an emotional faculty, arising from the astral plane, as
well as a lack of spiritual understanding.

It also can be a trap! It enslaves one to that which he
wishes to "belong to" and it may entail many lifetimes
before he can cut himself loose from the entangled
web of "belonging." In other words, the attitude of
following the pack or keeping up with the fashion world
or the Joneses down the street.

On the other hand, if the individual can maintain a
valued interest in another person, his community,
politics, religion or whatever makes life fulfilling to him,
but with inner detachment, the relationships involved
have a much greater chance of reaping happiness. To
become friends with detachment may not be as easy
as it sounds; however, it is one of the tools spirit gives
us for our spiritual unfoldment. We can "belong"
without "belonging to" any person, cause or pack, as a
herd animal. Yeap! I am giving most of the human race
the benefit of the doubt.

I have a large file of letters from people around the

world that contains the outpourings of sorrow and sadness in their relationships with their mates and/or lovers. Marital breakups, jealousies, third-party situations, and very often with children standing squarely in the middle of the fracas, lead to very real suffering and pain for those involved.

One wife was complaining because her husband wanted her out of the teaching she was studying in Menlo Park, California, and out of her job with her parents. Her first line said it all: "Right now, I feel angry!" She was satisfied with her spiritual life and had no problems with her parents or working for them and she was "tired" of having to do battle with the man she had married. She was seriously attempting to balance out the situation in her life rather than walk away from her husband. Another young woman was desolate because "I am not lonely due to the presence of the master, but I feel a longing for this man and I suffer when I know I cannot see and be with him."

And when this young man lost his lady, "I missed her so much I felt ripped apart in infinite agony at loving her, for all I could see was this causing me misery. I loved her as much as I was capable, and I know that love was real love, but it was not good for me. I have no intention of ever missing anyone that much again."

From another: "I have been grieving over a broken dream, to be happily married to a kind, intelligent man who would care about my feelings, be a loving companion, and sexually faithful to me. That is the dream I married almost 16 years ago, but as life, luck and karma would have it, the man I married did not have the same dream for himself."

A young man who was in the Army and stationed overseas, learned that his young bride had become pregnant by another man. Although deeply hurt by her unfaithfulness, he brought her overseas with him so they could raise the child together. While wanting to be understanding and loving about the situation, he is hurt inside that she conceived another man's child, not his own, yet he will heal fast with the aid of the spiritual assistance of the master.

There are ways individuals can rise above their problems and not be affected emotionally by them. I have written and spoken of this many times simply because it is such a widespread problem among men and women. They can develop a perspective and perception, subjectively and objectively, that can lead them into a much richer and fuller life, without that guilt factor that is impressed upon mankind by society, man's religion, and the materialistic world we live in on this planet.

It is quite common for mates to be possessive of each other, to be dominant in their desires for their companions, to allow very little freedom for the others in their lives. Most often this individual is basically immature in his dealings with others for emotions are very hard to control. The emotional state is connected with the astral plane, which is the heaven area for many orthodox religions.

These individuals cannot give love to those dear to them, but man must love something, his work, family members, humanity or God in order to survive spiritually. But if permitted within his space, the spiritual traveler can gently probe and pry the coiled springs of disturbed emotions to bring him into the positive action of love. Part of the problem with anyone going forth and building a spiritual foundation here in this world is that he must somehow allow some outflow.

As one goes forth in life one recognizes that an idea, an impulse for a thought, is issued out of soul, transmitted from God to the mind via spirit in the waking or dream state. It flows through an individual and then is sent out through the spoken word or expressed in some other manner.

Isn't it true that one, or all, again and again contact that area of originating thought? Within heavens (the metaphysicians think of it as Universal Mind), this area is known as the Ocean of Love and Mercy.

When an individual has come forth with an idea, then sends it out via the mind, it does not follow that it is his or her particular possession.

If one did appropriate and hold onto it, how can there be room for receiving more understanding, let alone knowledge of God, heaven, this universe or this world?

The initiate must recognize and realize, to receive more, one must give out what one has received, whether we receive it through the discourses, the books or through our spiritual contemplative exercises.

Some are fortunate to receive a direct knowingness of various aspects of life; others don't have that. Some have very vivid dreams, and knowledge is imparted and brought back, not in its totality but piece by piece for some as the consciousness in the human state can handle it. Other Initiates do not see but know, have no recall of dreams, no visualness in the lower worlds but only abstract forms during their spiritual exercises,

22

yet they are gathering this spiritual knowledge for which there is a longing within themselves.

It is a knowledge and a knowing truth that if we will hold what we receive from the spirit, stagnation sets in and we will be like the wheel of a mill that is turned by the stream to grind the wheat to flour, and suddenly of its own volition, begins to withhold the water which it was using. It will soon be stifled with inert water. It is only when the water is allowed to flow freely and push that wheel to create the power to grind the wheat that the end product is achieved.

The same is true with man. When we contact the spiritual force and the ideas that flow from God through us, we must give it out in order to receive the benefits from spirit. We must give it out to the rest of the world, to our friends, neighbors, loved ones, without forcing or being boastful, but tactfully, discreetly, with ease. One must allow all of his fellow men to do the same. That way one grows and develops as he is giving forth of oneself.

There is no argument about any of the past teachers that are ascended for all things are from God, and whatever someone, whether a spiritual teacher, savior or holy man has done, all men can do.

This includes women, for in soul, regardless of race, color, creed or sex, the miracles that some of the initiates who are women are performing are beyond the mental grasp of the average person on the street. One learns that the only requisite necessary for each individual is to be willing to let the spirit flow through, for God to express itself, without directing it towards any course. It is taught that through the teachings that all are created equally in soul, yet each of us as individuals do not have the same spiritual understanding nor spiritual unfoldment.

That in soul we are all One, and one comes into the understanding, as he pursues the teachings that are taught, that there is nothing mysterious about these works. The mystery is only in man's mortal concept of them.

I have spent various weekends at various Wisdom Temples during my training towards mastership. I had the pleasure of meeting all of the masters, as well as individuals, men and women, that work at the Wisdom Temples, assisting in many ways.

They carry out requests exactingly, with ease, with a poise and an attitude that all need to establish and as one continues on the path, eventually establishes. They accomplish their task in a way surpassed by very few people here on Earth or in the rest of the worlds, with pride, dignity, loyalty, without the slightest question or criticism.

I remember one afternoon that Fubbi Quantz had given some orders to some individuals. I didn't hear a word spoken or see a piece of paper handed to them but the directive given was carried out in a very orderly manner.

All preparations were made for the coming visitor in such a businesslike arrangement that it was hard for me to imagine at that time.

Every detail was complete, everything put into line with a rhythm and precision of music. This harmony that was experienced was maintained throughout the entire afternoon, and during every visit that I made to any of the Wisdom Temples, I saw the same sort of performance. It was a pleasure that day, for the preparation was made for Yaubl Sacabi.

One of the men was well advanced in years and it appeared that he wouldn't be able to carry out any of the physical work that he was supposed to do, yet whether the individuals were younger or older, it didn't matter, their efforts were efficient with no bluff or bluster. Every order that was received verbally was monotone and then carried out with exact precision and sort of a quickness but yet with ease.

It is an individual's responsibility to unfold themselves spiritually, to keep their body in good working order and maintain it in harmony with the spirit. Every person in his right domain is limitless, for the masters and many of the initiates coming up in this era know no limits of time or space. For the individual, when he knows himself, is not obligated to toil wearily along for days on end to accomplish a certain task.

There is a law of spirit that what an individual expresses returns to him as truly as he expresses it. Therefore, one must learn to express only the good and the good returns to the individual only as good.

The masters, working for the good of the whole, keep this foremost in mind and use it to move about and throughout the ethers into the physical worlds, as well as into the various levels of heaven.

The things I do or any of the masters do, are accomplished in accord with a definite law and each person is able to use this law if he or she will only abide by its rules: These are the spiritual laws of spirit.

True, it takes many years of patience and spiritual

discipline on an individual basis to reach that level. Love of life and inner peace is what most of the masses have been seeking, and do not know where to find it.

On one of the many journeys with Rebazar Tarzs and Peddar Zaskq, in which I have visited a very special temple, and I wrote of it once before, I have seen many healed of all types of illnesses. The expression in this temple has been of the love of life and of the inner peace of the individuals, not only of those that built it but of those that go to it.

Ever since it has been built, its vibrations are so strong that most who go through this temple are healed immediately, if they have any afflictions or illnesses. However, one must keep in mind that they wish to be healed. The healings are due to the strong vibrations of HU that have been established there many, many centuries ago, and the HU continues to be sung from time to time by those who believe, who know, and who have been healed, including the masters.

Should any harsh word attempt to be stated, or any kind of harsh word be used, these thoughts would have no power, and it would be impossible for words to be uttered. This same principle also applies in one's life. Should you think and say kind words of love, joy of life, have harmony for all life in your heart, and keep perfection in soul, in a short time, man would be unable to say harsh or unkind words to his fellow man, let alone to himself, whispering under his breath about others, within himself. This same practice must take place within man's own sacred temple, at the temple within himself, for a daily session of devotion, of contemplation. The masters are then able to impart instructions, to avail themselves of this opportunity.

It is not always possible for the people of this world, or of other worlds, to reach the master, or any of the masters in the physical realm. This is why they are encouraged to go to the temple within, for understanding, healing and spiritual unfoldment.

All those who approach the master for help are greatly benefitted, including those who seek out the Living Master in the physical. Those who are curious and those who seek psychic experiences learn that the masters are ordinary men, yet they are super-human beings, due to the knowledge they possess.

Those individuals seeking that psychic experience are not given the insight that those who are sincere and believe they have a way which is unique, receive.

I have had a great number of people tell me verbally and in letters they were healed, for I know they declared silently that they desired to be made whole. From letters throughout the years, from some of the initiates around the world initiated by Paul Twitchell, and many initiated under my spiritual guidance, it was found that of those individuals healed at different times, with the proper attitude, ninety-percent had a permanent healing.

This is one of the beauties given to man, and it is up to him, the individual, to choose to use it or not to use the temple within. Why, you can go there as often as you choose without any cost to you in this costly, material world. All it takes is a little time on your part. It seems that down through the history of man, he has sought to create in stone, wood, silver, gold and brass that which he idolized and worshipped, whether it was in the form of ornaments, huge statues or items of structure in places such as museums. Items of this nature have very little to do with man's spiritual unfoldment, as they cannot be taken on to the other worlds.

This started at a temple within many centuries ago, from the pattern which was formed in the minds of those who went within, and the idea became fixed in the minds of these men. This led to the worship of idols.

In spirit, through contemplation, one is able to overcome the worship of any former idol. As the image is formed, one becomes conscious that the pattern surpasses the idol. The use of singing the HU, breaks up the pattern of such worship and replaces it with divine love.

Through spirit, this includes replacing the idolizing of the personality of others. We should idolize the divine spirit which expresses love and life, and not personality. What is stated here is that individually we must go to the temple within, clearly to live a balanced life. In doing so, should you be looking for a healing, do it with sincere belief. It will be so, for it takes spiritual visualization by the individual.

Emotions should not be suppressed nor should children be taught to suppress them. There are no bad or good emotions; they are only emotions. By one "controlling" emotions, if started at an early age, an individual becomes much stronger spiritually than the average citizen, for years are added onto his life. This is one of the secrets of longevity.

People in a depressed state of consciousness don't recall or remember how to lift themselves out of this depression into that state of spirit they once knew when they had freedom, not only of choice, but an inner freedom that was a stability.

One must learn to discipline himself in regards to his emotions, and not allow emotions to run rampant. He works with detachment which means to detach himself in his affections, innermost feelings and interests, and not to identify himself with his possessions and environment. When he becomes non-resistant to other people's moods, their emotional upsets and hatreds, he climbs upward in the world instead of sliding down.

This is not to say that we are emotionless and cold and aloof to members of our family. But since we are conditioned to live by our emotions and feelings, this can lead to irrationality and unreasonableness. Injury done to the emotions forms an aberration that may take lives to erase.

The more we use conscious detachment, the more we are working with one aspect of divine knowledge, and those who have a good working awareness of divine wisdom are usually extremely kind towards others. For they know the power they generate which can be used to help or harm depending upon the ethics of the individual involved.

Spiritual giants have often suffered at the hands of others rather than return the "eye for an eye" treatment to another, for they are aware of the damage they can incur with their powers.

29

The spiritually aware individual on the ladder to the Godhead will find it a lonely pathway, but in time greater strength is obtained, and he becomes more self-contained, not requiring friendship, love or special feelings from others except those he wishes to love or be with.

The state of human consciousness is under the command of the negative power, known as Kal Niranjan, or better known as the evil force, the devil.

It is kal's duty, given to him by the one God, the Supreme Deity, to restrain soul from returning to its home in the Godhead, to keep it so busy it forgets its basic purpose, which is to obtain experiences and training in the lower levels of the universes of God and return as a co-worker.

Not in a passive sense of becoming one with IT, but as an active co-worker on some level of God's worlds, working in a capacity of soul's own choice.

This is where kal has a heyday with religions in the East and West, having them think that they are working for God when all this time, they have been playing the hand of the negative force.

So kal sets up traps for soul, enmeshing it in thousands of lives to hold it here until it is purified and aware of its purpose.

This involves Self-Realization and God-Realization. Many of the traps used by the kal are the mind perversions: Lust, Greed, Vanity, Attachment and Anger, also known as the five passions of the mind, each with its own sub-category aspects. Objects of sensual desire, wishing for control and power, lusting for the things of the materialistic world, keeps one in bondage, a slave to the lower realms.

Pride, one of the worst manifestations of vanity, and false humility, the most common, swells the heart with self-righteousness and creates a mental carcinoma worse than any physical cancer.

Attachment to family, problems, illnesses, possessions, money, criticism, blame, etc., is the magnet that holds soul to the lower worlds. Until these attachments are neutralized and put in perspective, soul must continue returning to the worlds below the soul plane, life after life.

Anger is a highly destructive mind-action. Tantrums, slander, gossip, backbiting, profanity, fault-finding, jealousy, malice, impatience, resentment, destructive criticism and ill will fall under this insidious slave-driver. It can be seen how all five of these mind perversions are brought into play when the emotions rule the individual.

Man must learn to work in harmony with the laws of the spiritual worlds, the psychic worlds and the physical worlds. One of the great laws is to Love All Things and Love One Another. That doesn't mean to smother each other, but to love one another, and this divine love that is referred to here is an impersonal love that allows for the greatest spiritual freedom imaginable.

Perfection is not to be found in the lower realms of existence, yet man continually searches for perfection. Just as the woman wrote in her letter earlier, she went in search of a dream husband and a dream marriage but her dream fell through when she found it was not her husband's dream as well. She was unhappy with her lot in life because her dream did not come forth as fact,

31

and until she could face that her husband did not live up to her expectation of what she thought he should be, she had the choice of remaining in the marriage unhappily, or leaving the marriage and beginning a new life without him. But until she looked objectively at her image of what a husband should be, she might jump right back into the same situation with another man. The perfection she wanted did not exist in the man she chose to live with. He was working out his karmic ties with her and with others, and so was she.

They could probably come to some sort of understanding if they faced their truths about themselves and each other and tried to work things out between them. We should be more advanced in understanding than mice or rabbits.

The inner master leads us to the form of life necessary for our spiritual perfection and if we are in a situation we are unhappy with, it can be reexamined and changed to suit our preferences. However, if the individual remains cheerful, works harmoniously with whatever has been dealt him in life, he will find himself moving out of areas that infringe upon his world, the world of his making. Perfection in consciousness is gained as mechanicalness is destroyed. This is what the Initiate learns as he is taken through the inner and outer teachings by the master, who appears to the chela or student on the inner.

It is not enough to withdraw from life, for life allows for all growing experiences for the individual, yet each must take responsibility for himself and those responsibilities he has incurred in his daily living, such as his family and job, under the spiritual guidance of the master. The master is the example, via the will of God, for the initiate to use in his quest for spiritual perfection.

As the individual unfolds into spiritual maturity, something each and every individual must eventually do, he finds that he, man, the individual, the microcosm in the macrocosm, is capable of reproducing all the qualities of God, "the Over Soul" as Paul Twitchell called IT. The individual, on his own, must make his own way to truth. .

The gaining of detachment should not be construed as ignoring or turning a cold shoulder toward living, the family, community, job, etc. It can be misunderstood and some have felt that since they were on a path that could lead them into the heart of God, they no longer needed the association of loved ones or that which makes up their daily existence. Not true. The higher one goes on the spiritual ladder, the more ethical one becomes. One goes about his daily business, joyful in the knowledge he has received, and works out the responsibilities he has taken upon himself. One does not walk out on the family or one's mate or job, or community undertakings unless all are in total agreement with this departure.

We go through a certain amount of pain and pleasure but we no longer are pulled to the extremes of the emotional scale. We remain balanced emotionally. When thoughts are charged with emotions toward another person, he senses this psychically and will react to these thoughts even though they are never spoken. Fear and anxiety come across the same way, whether kept inside or not. By putting out sincere thoughts of good will for those around us, good will is received in return. This, incidentally, works just as well and as truly when thinking about your car, a plant, a piece of equipment, etc. Again--what you sow, you reap! Most of man's illnesses are emotionally oriented in cause, from the desire to control and dominate, as well as his diet. This is true of nations and religious orders East and West.

Behind this basic longing for "belonging" lies the law of love--divine, impersonal love for all things. Soul longs to return to its true love, the Godhead. It seeks and searches, not knowing why. It has become so enmeshed in the worlds of the lower kal regions that It has forgotten Its identity. It searches through Its body shields for a mate, peace, comfort, prosperity, contentment, and when these mind illusions are not forthcoming, It turns to despair through drink, drugs, dissipation. The exhilaration when one "gets religion" is the hope that the mysterious search is over, but most seekers go through one religious path after another before they find what seems to be the answer for them.

Soul may often spend many lives on various spiritual paths, moving closer and closer up the spiritual ladder toward the fulfillment of Its reality. Then when It is the weariest, and often at its lowest point, It is brought into contact with a spiritual guide and led to the master. The recognition of soul for its true self is mutually noted and the journey homeward to Sugmad begins. Karma is worked off the first two years through the guidance of the master, prior to the light and sound initiation. It may be easier for some to accept a living spiritual guide than

34

others, but if the individual is sincere in his desire to return to his home in the Godhead, to learn to retain his own individuality into and beyond eternity, or become one with God (an Atom in an atom structure), he will receive the help he needs.

The karmic ties that draw individuals to each other from past lives can be resolved and they may stay together throughout their lives by mutual agreement if they live harmoniously together and enjoy each other's company. Should they part, by maintaining good will and love for each other rather than anger and hatred, then no karma is built up or created in their separation.

The book, Stranger By The River, by Paul Twitchell carries this passage: "When ye love one another so great that it does not matter what the other does, then ye have unconditional love, and thy love has risen above the planes of this earthly world. Then ye know how to love me, thy God, and creator."

There is one important aspect we should not forget and that is this creative faculty that is within each and every human being. This is not the imagination but the creative force that flows through all life. Utilizing this creative force in getting yourself into the heavenly worlds beyond yourself can be very easy, provided the detachment faculty or the detachment from material things, and from one's loved ones is understood and used. The greater aspect of detachment is love for those who practice the higher, divine love do not talk about it, they demonstrate it. For they also have complete detachment from the little things in this world we humans hang onto within ourselves.

There is no way we can rush the gates of heaven,

because when that happens IT forces that door closed more tightly and you feel trapped or in prison. If you have that feeling of being imprisoned, that is the time in your spiritual growth that you want to start to use that creative faculty. Imagine yourself with your spiritual guide or with one of the ancient masters. See yourself walking in the green fields of the astral plane or hearing the rushing of the waters and letting go with that detachment from all things on the inside of your self. Then it can happen.

One who takes up the study is never pushed by myself or any of the masters unless you ask for it. Then you will only be pushed as far as you can without hindering yourself spiritually and upsetting yourself.

The masters are more than happy to assist and help one unfold to the next point, whether it is with the utilization of the creative force or the spiritual exercises. All things have already been given to the one who steps upon the path and all that one needs is the guidance by the spiritual traveler through the lower worlds.

Some already know how to shift their state of consciousness, which is like shifting the gears of a car. However, it is easier, swifter and doesn't take as much effort as shifting the gears in a car. It's very painless and very rewarding once you learn it and understand the simplicity of utilizing that divine aspect of spirit.

It is divine! All things are manifested through it. This teaching is not a welfare program and we earn our way in the physical world, as well as the spiritual worlds. This detached state that one must reach is an idealistic state, and it is often misunderstood for it does not mean to leave family, home and job. Life is to be lived to its fullest. For those who give to that which is known as Spirit in service or coin, without looking for anything in return, without strings, are given threefold or more in return.

Some seem to have more spiritual advancement than others but you will notice they don't do much talking about loving others or doing for others, they just quietly do it. Those who boast about it and talk it up to whoever will listen have much to learn about Spirit. The physical detachment and emotional patterns are best viewed with flexibility. If we aren't careful, we can get tangled up in emotional situations that drain the bodies. We can be involved with our surroundings but be detached emotionally.

By learning to control the emotional center, you will find you are calmer, have more control of your inner emotions and can be more creative in going beyond yourself or shifting the state of consciousness. The flexibility spoken of in regards to detachment allows you the choice of deciding whether or not you want to be brought into a situation that may involve emotions. When this starts to happen, then other things can take place in the heavenly worlds.

There will be visits to the Wisdom Temples on the inner planes with the master where one learns more than words can convey. Keep in mind this knowledge is the only thing you can take with you when you die here. There is a new sureness within yourself, where you stand with yourself and with your loved ones, or your fellow man. You can talk about any subject or situation at work or at home without getting wrapped up emotionally, and should you get emotional, you know how to let go of it and let it be.

It is at the mother's knee that the child learns how to become a greater human being. If the parent can discipline the child when the child needs it, and be firm, there is a greater love between them. It doesn't mean that because of the detachment love is missing; it is a greater love actually, greater than the emotional love.

Down through time people have been given certain portions of the message. That which is the divine spirit sustains all life and it is unique. Let IT use you. That's what a flower does. It opens itself up and says, "Here I am, do what you will with me." Whether it is in the desert, or the mountain, or in your flower box in the window or in your garden. The bee uses it; we use it in different ways and it is very useful to mankind, just as a lovely sight to see or a fragrance to smell.

We can be more useful to IT and to that creative force. The preachers today are preaching about having a miracle happen to you, but you perform your own miracles every day--for yourself and for others, but the initiate is unable to talk about it, because no one would believe it.

That is the beauty of it. The disciples of Jesus didn't understand what he was talking about. They wondered and were puzzled. He spoke about a portion of the spirit in the form of light and sound and tried desperately to lead the people of his day to the temple within.

A lot of what was written in the Bible was about certain individuals' dreams and how they were to handle themselves in the lower worlds.

There is a far greater portion of the knowledge of spirit made available in this day and age, and without anything being held back, except by your own state of consciousness. This is the beauty of unfolding and learning some of the secrets of God, for one becomes more fragrant and beautiful than any flower that exists in any of the worlds or universes, including the heavenly worlds.

While no individual is ever turned away from the path, it may be better for some individuals to not step onto the path but to study through the books and tapes, and not get into any of the teachings. The reason for this is not all are detached from certain physical and material things in this life and we cannot go any further until we learn this--it truly is an individual path.

Occasionally there is a rude awakening as a realization hits us, but most can withstand it and come through smiling. Even if a situation breaks your heart for awhile, realize the attachment you have for the situation and possibly even for the agony that comes with the broken heart.

Then when you do, something happens and that light shines through and that smile is there. Or you go on, perhaps not going overboard or becoming overjoyed, but controlling the inner emotions.

We want to be able to enjoy each other and when we get together at seminars and gatherings, there is always laughter, love, music and happiness. That's fine, for if you can have that moment of happiness, grab it. Hang on to it even if it is a moment or an hour a day, for in this world ruled by kal there is always someone who will come along and try to bring you down to their level of sadness.

Chapter 3

WHAT IS EVIL?

"For the purpose of defining the two main conflicts in man (which are commonly called God) meaning good and evil, or positive and negative, let us give them prosaic labels such as aggressiveness and passiveness, " Paul Twitchell told me at a seminar. "The scriptures say 'Resist not evil' and yet many will partake of evil such as hating when hated, and being angry when another is angry. The revelations of the holy books want man to give up bad actions and embrace good ones, but so few of them tell how to go beyond good and evil, how to transcend the bounds of morality and the Law of Karma."

Both the Law of Vibration and the Law of Karma are involved here. The principle of vibrations governs the wave lengths, outflows from planets, stars, thoughts, feelings, actions, music, sounds, colorings, heavenly bodies and general harmonics. Karma, which is cause and effect, inflow and outflow, comes under this principle for these laws are the influences shared by soul and the bodies it uses in the various planes of existence.

Knowledge is never concealed from the eyes of the masses, but the masses refuse to see, note, and understand the knowledge that is right before their noses. They get caught up in emotionalism, swept into the tidal waves of astral impulses under the guise of "good versus evil" and end up with someone else's considerations, not their own.

A file folder of collected newspaper and magazine clippings shows the crawling encroachment of religious leaders into the political scene in the United States.

The cover of the September 15, 1980 issue of Newsweek carried the word "Vote" with the "t" expanded to a large cross housing evangelist preacher Jerry Falwell's face.

Inside, on page three, under the caption "Born Again Politics," a blurb heralds: "A potent new political force has taken shape on the right.

Through mass mail and the electronic pulpit, evangelical activists are attempting to enlist the nation's 30 million to 65 million born-again Christians in an unabashedly political crusade based on fundamentalist morality," to make these United States a Christian state which would be the downfall of this nation.

On page 28, the article "A Tide of Born-Again Politics," carries the subtitle "Television preachers mount a controversial crusade to bring old-time religion into the voting booth," and "A New Christian Right: Seeking salvation in the ballot box as well as in the Bible," underscores a picture of Christian literature expounding the political trail.

Just what are they trying to do, start an uprising in this country ?

Falwell was not the only evangelist sharing the billing in this issue of Newsweek. Other spiritual leaders in the United States voiced concern:

"What seems to trouble some critics the most is the movement's inexorable reduction of religious and moral values into crude political options," the article continued.

"I would hate for evangelical Christianity to become a spiritual version of the National Rifle Association," says Dr. David Hubbard of the Fuller Theological Seminary, who worries about the possible exploitation of politically naive evangelicals. And whatever it does to evangelicals themselves, the effect on the rest of society could be devastating."

"If in order to be faithful you have to support a certain stand regarding Russia, what's the next step?" asks the Rev. Theodore Edquist of the First Congregational Church of Boise, Idaho. "It strikes at the very heart of the whole notion of religious pluralism and religious and political freedom."

But Falwell counters: "We're not religious fanatics who have in mind a Kohmeini-type religious crusade to take over the government.... We support the separation of church and state...we want influence, not control."

Why is he and other T.V. Bible stompers trying to run for the presidency ?

The only thing the Christians or any religious groups should do is influence one to know and understand God.

In the San Francisco Chronicle, November 22, 1980, Rabbi Alexander Schindler, president of the Union of American Hebrew Congregations, "linked recent flare-ups of anti-Semitism, in part, to statements by

43

religious fundamentalists."

Referring to Jerry Falwell and Rev. Bailey Smith, of the Southern Baptist Convention, Rabbi Schindler continued:

"When the head of the Moral Majority demands a 'Christian Bill of Rights,' when the president of the Southern Baptist Convention tells the Religious Roundtable that 'God Almighty does not hear the prayer of a Jew,' there should be no surprise at reports of synagogues destroyed by arson and Jewish families terrorized in their homes...

" I do not accuse Jerry Falwell and Bailey Smith of deliberately inciting anti-semitism," Schindler said. "But I do say that their preachments have an inevitable effect."

Twenty-five hundred evangelical Christian leaders gathered in Washington, D.C. following President Ronald Reagan's inauguration "to worship and to develop future strategy for turning the nation back to God."

Marjorie Hyer's article in the San Francisco Chronicle, January 31, 1981, went on to add that "Speaker after speaker portrayed the 1980s as 'the decade of the evangelicals,' a boom time for conservatives generally and particularly for those concerned with a return to traditional morality....

"The involvement of evangelicals--or, as Falwell prefers to call them, Christian fundamentalists--in politics was one of the themes at the numerous speeches, workshops and discussions."

President Reagan, who had been invited to attend but who did not, was mentioned in one telling paragraph:

"There were some expressions of disappointment both because Reagan did not show up and because of what the religious leaders perceive as his failure to pay political debts with appointments to his administration from the Christian right."

When religious leaders use their beliefs to elect officials to public office, they, like anyone else, expect these officials to follow through with their demands. The elected official is obligated to do so if favors are accepted.

When any group attempts to press its opinions and ideas on the whole, without the agreement or permission of the whole, that group is interfering with the psychic space of others.

This is a violation of spiritual law, primarily evoking the Law of Cause and Effect or Karma, where one reaps what one sows, and becomes the effect of that which he has caused to happen.

For Christianity to be used as a tool for politics is ignoring the basics of the Constitution of the United States. Many Christians abhor the idea of being manipulated by over-zealous evangelists who are not really concerned with the Will of God or they would not press their own wills upon God's creations.

Producer Norman Lear, with the support of the People for the American Way, a group of religious and lay leaders, placed three 60-second television spots to counter the "political exhortations of those evangelists who have become a controversial issue in Campaign '80," according to the publication Broadcasting, October 27, 1980.

The spots stressed "that there is no one 'Christian' way to vote..."

Is this not the same thinking as the cults of this world? What is going to happen to free thought and point of view should this take place ?

"Lear claimed that the People for the American Way, through spots and literature will continue after the election. He explained that his initial contact with the new right came while he was researching a movie that was to satirize the movement.

" 'It grew less amusing to me,' he explained."

Writer James Michener is "disturbed by the growing trend toward mixing religion and politics."

Interviewed for Republic Airline's magazine, Scene, November 1980, Michener explained, "Those people who are trying to dictate public policy from their religious beliefs are a very dangerous component in American life.

"We've seen in the Reverend Jim Jones in Guyana how a religious drive in the field of politics can turn very sour indeed,"... by using the cross and Jesus who did not even wish to be worshipped.

The Los Angeles Times carried an article by John J. Goldman entitled "Campaign Opens Against Religious News Right."

It spoke about a television commercial supported by a "new nonpartisan national committee" who deal not with "selling soap but with selling separation of church and state....

"If my preacher and I don't try to tell anybody how to vote, then nobody is going to try to tell us how to worship. After all, that is the American way, isn't it?"

46

Sardonic columnist, Andy Rooney, commentator on television's "60 Minutes," stated facetiously in a recent column: "Let's make the official religion in our schools and in our government Presbyterian," for...."freedom to pray in our schools would be compulsory."

How about just the 3-Rs? When one's feet get close to the fire, one learns how to pray quickly.

Summed up in Family Weekly, October 26, 1980, in an article entitled "The Power of the Christian Right," Lisa Myers stated, "The strategy of the conservative evangelicals is to use the air waves, the mails, the churches and even the pulpits to elect a government that is strongly pro-defense, anti-Communist, anti-abortion, anti-Equal Rights Amendment, pro-family, pro-school prayer and anti-homosexual."

Under the guise of "religion," so-called spiritual leaders are opting to hold a staff of power over mankind so the masses are coerced to do things their way. Separation of state and religion was brought into the Constitution of the United States to protect the individual from being forced to worship a certain way.

While a man's religious upbringing may mold his character and his standards, they should not be jammed down another's throat. Many a bloody war has been started in the name of religion or over the name of God. Why would mankind believe that their deity would want one of its own creations to annihilate another?

Guilt surfaces through the bids to help rid the world of grief, suffering, hunger, sorrow and woe. The "good" would automatically want these things stopped, but because man has forgotten his purpose for being in this world, he does not understand that he is manipulated into doing and saying what the media princes would have him believe.

There is a concentrated effort underway to make the United States a Christian-oriented country, with Christianity the state religion.

Where does that leave the individual who prefers another spiritual path? Will he once again be forced to leave his country to strike out for another shore where he will be allowed to worship God in his own way?

It is a frightening thing that is happening here and those in authority who have been elected to serve We The People, should never permit mass-religious zealots to use their wiles and ways to sway elections or push moral and spiritual matters through the laws of this country.

My forefathers, as most in this country of the U.S.A., came here just to get away from religious persecution.

No one can "save" another. If the religious leaders would content themselves with spiritual issues and leave politics to the men who serve their country as politicians, the jangling controversies would disappear. The truth is here for everyone to see and behold if truth is what they want.

The "gays," in their frenzy to come out of the closet, have alienated a lot of people who don't really care what their sexual preference is. But there are gay bars, gay resorts, gay parades, gay communities, and gay politics. Their desire to "separate" themselves from "straights" by forcing their "difference" upon the world creates sensationalism all the while they are decrying

their persecution. Once more, there is a misunderstanding of the spiritual laws. If the gays or the masses
understood these laws, then we would have a better
world to live in.

There was a time when something "gay" meant
pleasant, light and happy. Now it denotes a psychic
aberration that one learns will disappear in time, unless
it is hugged to the bosom.

The five mind perversions or passions, lust, greed,
anger, attachment and vanity are shifted out of the
consciousness of the individual who realizes his or her
true purpose, and who truly desires to return to the
Godhead as a co-worker.

One learns there is no shame, no guilt, no sin, and
understands his total sense of responsibility to himself,
his family situation, his job, his community and his
country. The world is not his oyster, but a stage upon
which he and his fellow beings perform their day-to-day
lives.

His ethics become higher and more refined than he
has ever known them to be, not because anyone
expects this of him, but because he learns that each
individual has to live his own life in his own way, and he
grants others that opportunity. He does not expect
someone else to take care of him or think for him or live
for him, and he does not fight anyone else's battles
unless he chooses to with their permission.

If his government presses a religious stand upon
him, he will resist it. He is not passive about someone
entering his psychic space without his permission, and
he will let the intruder know it, for anything forced into
the space of another, even subliminally, is like an

intruder who violates your home.

I speak out on issues that disturb me, not only as a master but as an individual. When one tries to use their teaching to get out of serving the draft in their country, I tell them they can't do this. They can object as an individual, but not under the guise of their spiritual path. I served my country (W W II), and so did Paul Twitchell, my predecessor. I didn't want to kill anyone, and I didn't have to. I was at the right place on the time track. It is possible to take responsibilities that come along in your life and handle them without harming another, but they can still know you are not to be trampled upon.

In one of my books, Your Right To Choose, I wrote about abortion being a woman's right, should she not choose to bear a child and take care of it until it is on its own. For the fetus does not become a sheath for soul, nor has one, until after that body form has come into this world. It is just a group of cells and not until the umbilical cord is cut from the mother, is the soul forced into its body. Soul uses the physical body to exist in this coarser vibration. If one physical body is not used by a particular soul, it will use another. It is here to have life experiences and is in no hurry. It will eventually find its way back to its origin--the soul plane, where it learns its true identity. It wears a protective sheath, the human body, a marvelous electro-chemical and mechanical mechanism with a built-in computer.

These views were expressed through a message placed by a religious Menlo Park, California Corporation in the Washington Post in the spring of 1981. It was in response to Christians who were lobbying in Congress to have a man and woman jailed if they chose to abort an unwanted fetus.

The reactions to this message, though not unexpected, were startling since it was men more than women who reacted against the message. Not so strange when it is realized that men originated the abortion hysteria to begin with.

How can women be kept "in their place" if they are free to make such choices about their own bodies? I doubt that women will permit this law to take effect, for basically it places them back in the dark ages where they were subservient to men and forced to do men's bidding.

The freedom that women have received in the last few years is not something they will give up lightly, even though it is cloaked under the mantle of "pro-life," or the fetus' misunderstood "right to life." It is a political ploy not a spiritual fact.

Moral issues tread the astral plane, the emotional sheath that clothes soul while it dwells on that plane, the first level of heaven. By infiltrating an individual's astral "home," religious leaders use emotional appeals to conditioned guilt feelings and harbored fears.

They can misuse their ability to reach others to obtain financial aid for "world hunger," to sway weaker individuals to their causes, to manipulate political leaders to front for their power plays, and all under the guise of religion.

When individuals realize they are being used in this way, they can resist the attempt to railroad them into avenues they do not wish to take.

Under the "good" and "evil" labels, those who feast

upon man's emotional atmosphere do him a great disservice. They will also reap the karmic burden they have created, perhaps not in this life, but in the next.

They will know the oppression they deliver to others' doors. But the enlightened individual does not have to permit this to happen. Truth is not hidden for those with eyes to see. But man has to develop that latent ability within him to go beyond his outer or physical state of consciousness or awareness.

Jesus knew how to do this. There is a part of his life that is left out of the scriptures. He received some of his early training amongst the Masters at the Katsupari Monastery in the Buika Magna mountain range of northern Tibet. He spent about nineteen years in India and Tibet. It is a known fact he went into India from his homeland, but when he went back from Tibet to India where he had great discussions, he was thrown out of India by the Brahmans and returned to Jerusalem under the guidance of one of the Masters of that time, Zadok.

Whether you believe this or not, and many do, Jesus set up his conditions himself. He could have prevented the crucifixion but he chose to go through it. Many in the world look to Christmas day as the birth of Jesus and have been taught that he was sent here to Earth to die for our sins. One learns that the only "sin" there is, is the "sin" we create for ourselves.

We can spend a lifetime trying to develop the physical body but it is not necessary to move it about and take it into the ethers. There is a greater body to develop and that is the Soul. It is unlimited and It cannot be harmed.

Jesus wanted to show the masses that there is a heaven. For this reason he walked upon the water, but it wasn't with his physical body. He manifested an astral body, which is a direct duplicate of what you see in the physical, and what the soul body can be that has this ability to manifest Itself.

Many think of Jesus as God. Many appeal to him as a mediator between them and God. Some Christians I've heard voice their stern opinion or they seem at times to think of God as being angry, sitting off somewhere in a place called heaven located in the sky, perhaps. They do not know it lies in man's consciousness and within his own heart. The Christians and those who look to Jesus seem to be able to reach God only through his less austere way. The masters recognize Jesus, Buddha and other great teachers on this Earth planet but do not commemorate or celebrate their lives as man has all these past years.

In Jesus' situation, the Christians think of him and call him Christ. It is a state of consciousness. He was a good teacher. Very few understood him. He attempted to liberate the uninitiated in his day from the material bondage and limitation of this Earth. His mission was to show the people of his time more fully the way to the real God, the one source, the great omnipotent, omniscient and omnipresent One. To show that God, Sugmad, was all-goodness, all-wisdom, all-truth, all-knowing.

Buddha and Jesus also attempted to show more fully that God not only dwells without us but within us, that IT never is or can be separated from us nor any of its creations, that it is always a just, loving and exacting

God. That through spirit, which is its vehicle of communication and knowledge, it knows all things, knows all that is truth. It does not matter if those who doubt don't believe that Jesus got his training from the Masters at the Katsupari Monastery. You can think of his training coming from the Masters as a direct revelation from Sugmad, the one Source, where all things really exist.

Prayer did not work well for me, and meditation keeps the individual in a passive state of consciousness. I knew whenever someone prayed for me and it bothered me inside. Most of you have gone through this or are aware of the feeling. It is an infringement on your own world. I was led to the inner chamber, the temple within. It took a lot of testing, a lot of hard work on my part, and a lot of experience from childhood on up to now. No one proselytizes on this path that few can walk, for this direct path to God is not for everyone.

But the initiate "knows" through his inner experiences, and becomes far removed from the traditional conditioning carried over from his past lives. He learns that he has created the problems in his life through the impersonal spiritual Law of Cause and Effect, the Law of Karma. There is one exception to this and that is, what others may dump upon a person behind his back. While he can help his neighbor if it is mutually acceptable, he would be foolish to carry the neighbor's burden when it is the neighbor who has accrued the burden in the first place.

Through abortion and birth control, the world's poor would not be hapless breeders of starving children the rest of the world is expected to care for. The "poor" could pull themselves out of the restrictive conscious-ness that keeps them "poor." When someone writes me for help with "my blood pressure," it shows the attitude of the individual who hugs that ailment to himself. They have accepted it as a possession, one they may not want to give up.

The only "shortages" in this physical realm are the shortages placed in the collective world conscious-ness by those who expect to benefit by the control they receive over others. Mankind only limits itself. The person who maintains an attitude of limitlessness has all he needs in his life, with enough left over to help out when necessary. This path is not a spiritual welfare program, for first you serve (put assets in the bank of life) before you can receive (withdraw from earnings).

This, again, is the spiritual law; however, keep in mind just how will you serve spirit ? You must take your time and have a firm understanding of the spiritual laws of the light and sound first.

Think in terms of how you act with someone--what kind of re-action do you receive back? This is true in thoughts as well as deeds. We are each now the by-product of all the lives we have ever lived. If you don't like your life, you can change it--for the better. But it takes some effort on your part.

When we experience and know the truth, the lie, and it is properly interpreted, is it not all from the same source--"Soul"? You may ask if we believe that death is avoidable?

Our human body is constructed from an individual cell, like the bodies of animals and plants which are less evolved states of consciousness. As you know, the

individual cell is a microscopic unit of any living body.
The process of growth and division is repeated many
times, to build up millions of countless cells into a
complete animal, plant or human being. These body
cells are specialized for certain body functions, yet
they retain the main characteristics of the individual cell
from their original source.

This transfers from generation to generation,
originating from the level of heaven known as Soul.
With this in mind, the vitality of all living beings has an
unbroken ancestry which reaches back in time before
life existed on this planet Earth. Keep in mind that the
individual cell has the uniqueness of unlimited growth.

The age of the most ancient of the Masters who still
teaches in his same body today, Yaubl Sacabi, is
beyond human conception. For it is said that he could
be over 5,000 years old. There are a number of
masters who have retained their physical bodies to
work for the good of all mankind.

Have you thought of a tree, flower or animal, let alone
another human being as your brother or sister ? Think
of the vital process going on in a flower or tree, as well
as yourself, which is fundamentally the same.

Look at the life reactions of a plant as well as yourself,
as being alike; we as human beings surely can profit
from this. The cells in man's body do not necessarily
need to gradually lose their vitality and decompose,
but may grow young as the individual cell itself.

As one learns this, there is no reason why one's
body should not grow young and vital as the young cell
from which it came. We as human beings derive from
the Divine Source, the twin pillars of God, the Light &

Sound, and must take an active part in this source, starting with the Light, which is knowledge, using the practice of the spiritual exercises, for all are very necessary.

There is no natural law of death nor decay for man; there is but one exception, which is accident. As Paul Twitchell pointed out in his writings, there is no inevitable old-age process which exists within the body of man or his cell groups. Senile decay of man, which is the common experience of man, is the expression of his ignorance of Cause, along with the diseased conditions of his mind which controls the body functions.

On this path accidents are avoidable with the proper mental attitude. With the practice of the spiritual exercises, the tone of the body can be preserved so it can naturally resist the infections and other diseases with ease. Keep in mind that youth is Sugmad's seed of love planted in each human body divine. This is why I speak to each as "young man" or "young lady," for youth is life spiritual. As Paul Twitchell pointed out to me at one of our meetings at the Top of the Mountain, he said: "It is life only which lives and loves the one life force, eternal." So don't sit in a corner--jump into the stream of life's daily activities.

Man is just ignorant about fear thoughts, for many are placed upon him by the various religions, news media and those who write about sin, fear of God and guilt. Thoughts of pain and grief are the creators of what man calls old age. Through the teachings, one learns that thoughts of love, joyfulness and cheerfulness bring about the beauty of youth. Age in the outer shell is not the gem of the true reality which lies within; the real fountain of youth is in Soul.

As stated in this teaching, as well as man's scriptures, we must be as little children. This is in a state of consciousness. We must learn to smile such as a child smiles, in a sweet way, from the heart, not the head.

The true smile is an action of true beauty and spiritual relaxation. We must also let go of thoughts of envy, hate, and the little things the mind wishes to always argue about. A child will not hold onto past moments. We also must let go.

The masters have taught to love one's self as well as his fellow man, to make the world a bright and beautiful world as well as to cultivate the spirit of humor. The teachings and the masters, are the oldest known. Their teaching antedates all history by millions of years.

The master worked with one person at a time, as well as gathering a small group who would listen, to try and show them a better way of life.

Long before man knew the simple art of civilization, it was from their teaching that the system of rulers sprang. However, the rulers wandered astray from the realization that it was the essence of God expressing itself through each of them. They thought it was themselves, the personalties, who did the work. They lost sight of the divine spirit, forgetting that all comes from one Source, God.

Chapter 4

LAUGHING IS HEALTH

Happiness and cheerfulness are survival factors.
Humor and the ability to laugh at one's self with others
is a very necessary factor in survival. It would be a very
sorry world if we weren't able to laugh once in awhile.

The survival I'm speaking of is beyond this world and
into the heavenly worlds and beyond eternity. If I make
an error, I'll admit it, and when it appears to be a
negative situation, make it positive.

When I attended my first seminar some years back to
see what the people were like, it was pleasing to see
the individuals were happy, yet there was a serious
side. The majority of them had a smile and an air about
them no one else has out there in the world. This love
of life just floats around and you feel it and want more
of it; it makes one at ease.

From childhood on up to this point I have learned that
in order to stay young, one must laugh occasionally,
whether he's laughing with nature, at himself, or with
someone else. The happiness of the initiate flows from
the pure, positive God worlds through the various
channels. I'm not the only channel for God. There are
others out in the world who open themselves up to this
Spirit and let it flow without directing it, such as some
artists or musicians, etc. Being a channel doesn't mean
that you are not going to take charge of your own life

during the day and guide your life the way you want it to be guided and not let others guide it for you. This is the whole program of letting the individual spiritually unfold himself into becoming what he wants to become, yet with a little happiness. If he can have a little bit of happiness during a twenty-four hour period, fine. This is part of life.

All of life is spiritual. A person digging a ditch may not like it, but if that individual has some initiative within himself, he's not going to be digging ditches all his life. On the other hand, a certain individual might be happy doing just that and enjoying it. There's nothing wrong with digging ditches. We can't set aside one day a week and say we're going to be spiritual on that day alone. One should live every moment as a spiritual moment, and if one is not, he is missing something.

The initiates are taught that regardless of who they are, where they are, and what they look like, there is no difference among us other than our outer appearance. In soul, there is no difference. We are all the same and from the same Source.

There's a great misunderstanding of the spiritual life among men of Earth. If torn between what is spiritual and what is material, the individual who doesn't really know should seek that answer within himself. The answer will come. Money is only a means of exchange for services rendered. It has nothing to do with spirituality. The various religious groups East and West are using you to get you to dig deeper for your dollars. They do it for their own concern, not for God or Jesus. I like to work with the underdog, in a sense, the person who is downhearted, the man of the street who hasn't made his niche in this life. I don't spend time with the person who has all the money and the material things in life, unless he has a spiritual problem. Then he'll show up.

If I don't have a penny in my pocket I'm rich, but that stems from some of the things I was taught as a little boy at my mother's and father's knee. Just look at the countries that are dominated by the church. They are very poor; the church wants it that way. The people of these countries proliferate and expect the rest of the world to feed and clothe them. This was taught to them by the missionaries.

There is one main purpose of life that mankind has forgotten: to manifest God in truth and in the spiritual laws that are a part of his learning experience. It is through ignorance of these laws that the individual runs into difficulties. When traveling in a foreign country or a state outside of your own, it is understood that you abide by the traffic laws and that ignorance of the state's laws are no excuse. This is true in the spiritual worlds as well.

We do not actually "create" our own families. We are distributing agents for spirit to flow through and it uses us as vehicles to bring souls into the world, and the individuals who bring a child into this world are responsible for it, not you or I or the rest of the world.

This creative urge is very strong; the factor of morals and society's rules were developed to maintain order. Spirit is the great forming power with which man can work in cooperation as a reflecting unit. When man misuses such attributes, however, he pays the consequences. That is the spiritual law. Whatever you hold in your mind is bound to come into existence sooner or later. No effect can come into manifestation without its originating cause. You bring a child into this world, you must feed, clothe it, give it a spiritual understanding and see it through school so it will not be a burden to society.

Perhaps the parents who put their child up for adoption are not involved karmatically with that child. They may be used as distributing vehicles to bring a soul into contact with the earth plane and through the overall plan of life, that child comes into contact with the individuals who do carry a mutual karmic tie with the child. It may be an unnecessary error of judgment for the adopted one to try to locate its biological parents for the karma may not lie with them.

The life and substance of the universe is derived from the pressing forward of the divine spirit for expression through the individual or the life forms that inhabit this universe. It is this formless forming power or substance that is "creation"--already in existence and awaiting expression. When the individual knows and understands this creative law and works hand in hand with spirit cooperatively to do its will, it cannot work antagonistically toward him.

We all have the choice of working as a channel for either the psychic force (Kal Niranjan) or that known as the divine spirit. When ethics and a sense of responsibility enter into one's consciousness, one will realize which force he is knowingly being a vehicle for.

There is no original sin as man has been taught, for he creates it as he lives life. Many people go through life with a great guilt feeling of sin, the sin of another person or of Adam and Eve.

The initiations help clear up this guilt feeling that most of the human beings experience. Someone wrote a good story about the original sin to control the masses of their time, and it has been handed down throughout history.

What do you expect out of life? What do you truly expect here and now?

Many people go through life wanting a better position and more of the things in this world, but they haven't stopped to think of how they are thinking about themselves, within themselves. You can go to all the colleges and get all the degrees that man can offer, and there's still that longing or yearning to know more about the far country, the many rooms in God's heaven.

Be inquisitive! I've always wanted to know where I'm going, and I found out. Keep an open mind; do not judge others by what you see, hear or read until you have the complete picture.

We are taught to trust in God, which is great, but we should trust that which is here within our midst, wherever we go, that sustains us as human beings which is spoken of as Spirit--the essence of God, its vehicle. It is the vehicle that carries out the creative yearning within us. We are its distributing agents whether we are aware of this or not.

Down through time, many of the great teachers have spoken of the far country, some of them mystics of all tongues and nations. Yet the religions have suppressed it because they want control of the masses, in a sense.

Guilt and fear are the weapons that are used to control mankind, unless one awakens to his true identity as soul and his true purpose, to become a conscious co-worker with the Supreme Being.

There is a vast amount of knowledge that far exceeds the understanding of man. When you transcend the physical body the only thing you can take with you is your inner experiences and that which man calls knowledge. But it is not academic knowledge.

Academic teaching and knowledge is good up to a point--to sustain yourself, to make your way in the world. That is your responsibility, not your parents' or what comes from your previous ancestry but it is up to you, yourself. Many people lean upon the past and have little success, or wait for their loved ones to die in hopes they will leave them their lot in life so they can have a good time. They feel they have all of the positive powers going for them, but sooner or later they have to pay.

Everything within the physical, material universe must be either earned, worked for, or paid for in some manner. This is from the etheric plane on down to the physical universe. This is a law of the lower worlds, a law of creativity.

We are taught that all we have to do is ask for something and it will be given, and sometimes this is true. But balance must reign while one resides within the physical realm or the lower worlds. You can seek and you will find, but you will have to pay for it. This you do not have to believe and I'm not asking you to, because man-made laws and universal laws of action and reaction exist.

Experiences you have had and some you will still have can gain you a greater understanding, a greater knowledge and wisdom not only for yourself but of the higher worlds. Learning how to get there and what you are going to do is totally up to you. The Living Master can only give direction and point the way.

You can partake of that nectar, that wine of God that you want to share with the whole world. Once you have it, you don't know how in the world you're going to share it, because spirit of itself is so vast the joy of learning about it overwhelms the mind. IT has created and sustains all life within all of God's worlds.

This is spoken of as the Bani, or the Shabda, and known as the sound current or audible life stream. It can be seen as light.

Light is knowledge and with knowledge of light alone, you can gain all life. Yet it takes the sound current to get you directly into the God-conscious state while here or on one of the lower planes, and it takes the Master to give that to you. Once you have that, you are well on your way to developing yourself to a greater human being than the man out in the street can comprehend.

It is a well-known statement that "like attracts like," therefore, those who seek materialistic solutions in life attract one another. It is a spiritual law, for good attracts good, and evil, or the lower consciousness, will attract its kind. The individual who desires more out of his life should give consideration to the thoughts he is attracting to himself.

Are they of a positive nature? Or is he constantly complaining and criticizing others?

This forming power called Spirit brings forth impersonally whatever is impressed upon it; therefore, if the cause is positive, so will be the effect.

Likewise, if the cause is negative, so will be the effect that comes about at some point in time. Not necessarily right away, although one will find that effects are immediate because of the spiritual energies he is working with.

The kal or negative force is very necessary in the workings of the physical plane world, since it is the negative pole of creation. We cannot escape the illusions of the negative worlds as long as we live here but we can be aware of them, understand them for what they are, and rise above them.

Animals work more in harmony with the lower plane laws than man does. They would seem to be smarter in their judgment, for by yielding to and working with the laws of nature, they adjust themselves to what they sense is useless to fight. Man will fight to the bitter end to outwit nature by what he calls "progress," and many times in the name of Allah, Jesus or God.

The positive pole of creation lies above the psychic worlds in the soul plane. The positive power is polarized in the master, via his inner and outer bodies, reaches and works with every chela on the path.

It is his prime function to bring those souls who ask and are ready back to the Godhead. Spirit of itself actually chooses us as individuals to go through the tests and trials to bring us to this state of understanding.

When working in a cooperative way with this divine flow, the individual who takes on the responsibility of mastership over himself will be tested time and again to see how he handles this responsibility. We establish our own set of values that work well for us, for man can be a law unto himself.

Always there is the matter of responsibility, for whatever man puts out to others creates a wave that will certainly ripple back to himself. Rarely will this affect him alone. Usually it involves family members, co-workers at his job, his community, and his spiritual life. In groups this works collectively and individually. The Mahanta (the Inter Master) will stand back and let the individuals have their experiences when there are lessons to learn.

When one changes his locality, his position or a relationship, it does not necessarily mean that he will have peace of mind, prosperity or security. Should he succumb to the siren call of the negative force, he will find it hard to resist unless he has a strong sense of self-discipline.

It is the duty of the kal power to hold soul in the lower worlds until It is purified and ready to move on into the higher worlds.

We may have experiences where we do not recognize what is happening on the subjective side of us, in our inner lives. It is very subtle but as the consciousness expands, we become more aware of what is happening within ourselves.

Our thoughts and feelings inside are very crucial to how we are going to function, not only here but in the spiritual worlds as well.

How can you tell a spiritual experience from a psychic experience?

A spiritual experience fills you with love, while a psychic experience may either frighten you or upset your whole foundation and give you a negative feeling. It may shake you for days.

The mind is a vehicle for the negative force; it is negative in nature. It is a useful tool but a tyrannical master of the dark force when in control. Man should master it, not vice versa. Spirit dictates the experiences one should have for unfoldment as one sets forth on any spiritual path but sometimes we let others set situations into motion that involve us, and we may have to control that. If we don't stop these situations, they are going to happen.

The initiate learns not to hang on to past moments. This is what is confusing to the mind as well as to others.

In trying to have some degree of understanding of why you are holding on to a thought implanted by someone else or one you haven't been on guard against within yourself, the mind becomes confused.

So many have experiences and do not recognize or realize what is taking place. We must keep a balance in our daily life. It goes from our thoughts within ourselves to our outer actions, not just what we say and do, but all of our actions.

A young man by the name of James Watt used to sit by the hour at the hearth in the large open-faced fireplace of his home, watching the steam come out of the cooking pot his mother was preparing for dinner.

He wondered how he could convert that to energy to help mankind. He was contemplating, not in a trance, but out of the body physically when his family would try to talk to him. He was thinking of how he could be a vehicle for the good of all.

Alexander Graham Bell and Samuel Morse also worked with this creative fluid, this forming power we call spirit.

To be a vehicle for IT is a responsibility. Many experience daily the light and the sound, the audible life stream, going into the pure positive God worlds with the guidance of the spiritual travelers, and enjoying life and happiness wherever they can.

In my travels I have found that in certain parts of the world there are individuals who rely upon and have a direct communication with the inner master, whether it be in the dream state or their contemplative spiritual exercise or when just walking down the street. They can ask a question, turn loose of it and if it is to be fulfilled, spirit fulfills it. If it isn't, they understand it wasn't meant for this moment of time.

Despite our modern technology with the microwave communications which are sent directly and swiftly from one point to another, and the laser, as well as telephone communication transmitted via copper wire and beamed around the world via satellite, the majority of the people within the world still have a very great hurdle to overcome. That is, to relax and learn to get their answers via the temple within.

There are great changes not only on this planet but elsewhere within the universes and worlds, those worlds that exist beyond this galaxy. Most of us have come from and have been in this world and galaxy for some time, but the initiate recognizing reincarnation, won't be likely to return to spend another lifetime on planet Earth, for they have the choice and the opportunity to have that direct knowingness of where they are going when they reach the end of the road in this lifetime. They may have knowledge of this from dreams or from their spiritual exercises.

I'm often asked what type of occupation an individual should get into, or if someone should change their occupation to another, but I have nothing to do with an individual's choice of physical jobs. The individual who wishes the spiritual assistance of the master can receive it, and if one knows that his spiritual life and unfoldment are taken care of, eighty percent of his worries are eliminated.

Letting an individual make up his mind whether or not he wants to take a certain step, whether it be in marriage, a job, a community decision, or on a spiritual path, is most important for no one can make his decision for him. There will be consequences to pay if we do.

The wisdom is not going to be given to you. It is earned. The experiences that one has, whether in the dream state or right out here objectively or during the spiritual exercises are also earned.

Sometimes they will come out of the blue when one isn't expecting them. Many have the experience of seeing the blue star and riding out with it, and going with it may take you into the pure positive God worlds. Those wanting to have psychic experiences on this path are only looking for discouragement. Some will have them because they need it for experience within the lower worlds, be it in the astral, or in the mental worlds. This is between the individual and what he has earned.

We as individuals get caught up in a pattern and it's a human trait. It's been handed down from generation to generation, and the masters are not involved in trying to break up these patterns, whether it is within an individual, a nation or within the world.

Change, whether it is in ourselves as individuals or in a country is very healthy. Without it we are not progressing. Whether it is on a moment to moment basis, day-to-day or year-to-year, we get into ruts. And these are karmatic patterns which many in the world try to break up, forcing changes upon the masses or individuals without their permission.

We tend to let the influence of past teachers or leaders in society guide us to some degree, and this tends to shape our daily activities and our karmatic patterns. We do not need to lean upon these individuals to form our daily habits.

Those who follow this path, find that they have a spiritual freedom that the rest of the world does not have. This freedom is a spiritual freedom of being able at a split-second's notice to rise above time, space and matter, and not be affected here in this physical realm.

This comes from practicing the presence of the master, and the spiritual exercises. If one can take from twenty to thirty minutes out of his day to establish that inner connection with the inner master, his day-to-day life will have greater meaning, with his spiritual life being cared for by the inner master and he handling his own outer life.

This essence of God, known as spirit, is very exacting and very gentle. Those not familiar with the spiritual exercises will find them far different from meditation or prayer or any other form of worship. For they are the highest form of worship, going to that temple within, but this is only a starting place. In the sound current which spirit supports, the sound waves are those one can ride upon to any part of the physical universe or any plane of existence. These other planes I speak of are part of heaven.

It is stated, not only in the Golden Wisdom Temples but in many other writings and discourses, that when the individual steps on this path, they are taken as swiftly as possible through the lower worlds from the physical plane of existence. For the masters in the Golden Wisdom Temples wish to move the individual on to the next temple. Yet no student is able to get to these temples without the guidance of the Living Master. You may not see him, but he is there.

When a person has earned the right, whether he goes for the writings of the master or to read the books in the temples himself, it's quite an experience for those who have the opportunity, not only to see it and experience it in the soul body, but also in the physical.

There have been a few that have been given this experience. It can be compared to watching a big television screen, and you are either in your home or in your office, consciously aware of what you are doing and where you are in the soul body.

It is a very free and enlightening experience, far greater than cosmic consciousness or the Christ-conscious experience that is gained by the different religious paths similar to self-realization. Their followers are not taken to the wisdom temple.

Once the master chooses to translate (die) when he has completed his tour of duty and the function in which he has taken on that responsibility, he works with those Initiates he has initiated and does not take on any further Initiates. He completes the cycle with each and sees them through the lower worlds. This does not mean he is a lesser power or that he has lost any power, as man thinks of power.

When a past teacher or leader has passed on, he is unable to assist individuals on this plane of existence except those he has initiated and only at the temple within providing one can reach him. He does not wish to come back to or return to this lower vibration once he has moved into the higher vibrations. There are masters who do not have to remain in this world and yet do, working from the wisdom temples here in the physical and all the universes that exist.

These masters work with the chelas who are brought to the wisdom temples, lecturing and assisting in their spiritual development. When these chelas read the books on each of the planes in the wisdom temples, they find it breaks up habit patterns that they have adhered to and either brought into this life from past lives, or generated during this lifetime.

Chapter 5

ENLIGHTEN YOURSELF

There have been in the past various initiations into mystical paths on this planet. Not only in this day and age but prior to man's origin here on Earth, there have been initiations into the teachings of the ancient masters. The initiations in spirit are a supreme distinction for anyone coming from other teachings seeking the true realm of God. When one passes through the initiation ritual, it will bring about the manifestation of the sacred forces to lift him into the supernatural realities of God. It is a positive experience unless you are thinking otherwise. However, keep in mind it takes self-discipline and your own individual initiative, nothing else, providing you have the spiritual guidance of a master.

Human beings will listen to anyone who is ancient and partake of any teaching if it is old, and while Judaism claims four thousand years of teachings on this planet, they do not have anything to offer their following like the direct experience of the true God worlds. It is a young child compared to the teachings of the ancient masters. There is only one master at a time who holds the rod of power. Do not take anyone's word for it, prove it for your self.

Those individuals who take the initiations are partaking of the audible life stream, the light and sound of spirit. Some can get into the light and sound without doing the spiritual exercises, for not everyone has to do them. It is up to the individual to use them to resolve his problems or difficulties, one way that one can help himself.

Generally a initiation is given after one to two-year study of the books and/or the discourses, either the class or of personal study. Occasionally some individuals are brought up the spiritual ladder a little sooner because they are ready and in some cases needed to hold a class or function somewhere in helping to spread the message. But getting that spiritual foundation is very necessary to accept what spiritually comes later, and to be prepared for the greater mysteries which are far greater than man with all his books and scriptures. With this preparation you can handle what is coming your way, if you take your time and go at your own pace without pushing and thinking the teaching is not advanced enough for you. All I can say is: Just keep going!

There are a few who will not want to take the second initiation after their two consecutive years of study time, having heard negative comments about initiations. When one has this kind of an attitude about such things, they miss one of the greatest opportunities in life--to unfold spiritually and work toward Self- and God-Realization. If someone else has had an unpleasant experience, it does not mean you will also. That was his experience, not yours, and comes from the attitudes and situations from his past, not yours.

The first year or two years of study are a preparation

and some of this takes place in soul on the inner planes in the Gobi desert. Some of the chelas who step on the path have been attending these classes in their soul bodies. The class size is about 125 students.

From there you move to a class room of about 75 students at the Katsupari Monastery in northern Tibet, again attending in the soul body. You work with the masters of the ancient order continually on through the lower worlds, up to and including the soul plane.

With the initiations presented, come responsibilities, but what you do with them is up to you; no one is going to push you.

Some can be trained to be teachers of the classes, some can use their creative abilities, like writing, artistic talents such as painting or with music, etc., but the message can be made available just by being a vehicle, a co-worker for God, wherever the individual is and no matter what he is doing or what he looks like.

There is often a misunderstanding about what takes place during the initiation. Before the individual knows it, the linkup to that divine current is made, for this takes place on the invisible side.

It is like giving one an enormous amount of energy and power. We are observed as to how we handle it, for the linkup to spirit will not be made if one cannot control himself.

To have that power and not know what to do with it is like one who has been given a large amount of money and doesn't know how to manage it. If spent wisely, it is always profitable. Just like sowing seeds in the ground, the preparation must come first.

The soil has to be worked, prepared, and then the

seeds sown. Once the seed is sown, it has to be cared for from that point on until it is harvested.

Gaining the conscious awareness of yourself, where you are at in this world and where you are going, can be done only by yourself. Others attempt to do this by forcing it with drugs or other artificial means, but there is no artificial way in which you can expand your consciousness into the God-conscious state while in the physical body or in any other plane of existence.

We cannot force open the spiritual eye (that spot between the eyebrows) for it must develop gently since the door to the inner worlds swings inward.

Many have made the statement that they have had an "inner initiation." Experiences on the inner are for the unfoldment of soul into greater awareness and are certainly steps on the path to spiritual unfoldment.

Inner experiences are treasured by those who travel the spiritual pathways, and should be as long as they are understood in their true perspective as steps upon the pathway. These must be confirmed by the law of spirit as discussed in the wisdom temples. The individual who has reached this inner initiation experience is being prepared for the next initiation.

It is important that the individual looking into the path read some of the books before taking the discourses, and then give sincere consideration to the commitment to his spiritual path before taking the initiations when they are offered to him.

They are not offered unless they have been earned. They are never to be taken lightly, but as a precious and sacred trust between the individual and his Creator.

There are worlds of duality where negativity exists, and there are the pure positive God worlds that one can go to once he has learned how. It is very simple but requires some self-discipline and practice of the spiritual exercises. Through the spiritual exercises we are able to grasp the different levels of heaven.

This requires sitting upright, feet on the floor, body relaxed, eyes closed, and looking sweetly into the spiritual eye. Place the attention on the master of your choice or that area between the eyebrows above the bridge of the nose. Then sing a sacred or secret initiation word, silently if with others or aloud if alone, or the name for God--HU--ten to twelve times, or Jesus.

Look and listen for a period of time, then sing or chant a word or verse that is uplifting for no more than twenty minutes to one hour. One gradually begins to raise his vibratory rate. The inner master awaits you and takes you to the wisdom temples or the inner plane experiences he might wish you to have. You may or may not be consciously aware of this encounter; it is very subtle.

Regardless of what part of this planet you walk on, that ground is just as holy as anywhere else--it is what you make of it. No one place is any holier than another.

It is what you do with what you have, but by regularly going to that temple within via the spiritual exercises, you gain an understanding and knowledge of yourself, and journeying in soul, what it means and what it can do for you. You will find that great areas of wisdom and knowledge can open up to you.

This is an individual path and will always be. The person with twelve initiations is no greater than the one who just stepped on the path, with the dream initiation.

Most of the former recognizes where the other individual is at and will neither boast nor put him down for he has a great awareness and becomes humbler. Those who act to the contrary are acting out of ignorance. When someone puts himself above another, he is deliberately trying to bring the other person down to his level of awareness.

Through the initiations some of the individuals, by developing themselves, can get into the area of the science of prophecy, which Paul Twitchell wrote about. When one builds a strong spiritual foundation with the creative techniques, the science of prophecy can be opened to him or her in the dream state or during the contemplative exercises.

I'm working with individuals rather than giving Akashic Readings, for they are time-consuming endeavors I do not have time for. It takes many hours to do a good reading. There are far too many others who wish to know more about the works of spirit.

Some view the light in their spiritual exercises, but others rarely see it at all. The most important factor is the sound, with thought the next important element for you move by thought from plane to plane in the lower worlds, through the astral, causal and mental worlds.

We don't make our own heaven in a sense, for it has already been made, but you set up conditions for yourself in these areas while you are here, or in the next life if you go to one of the lower planes.

The masters have, over the thousands of years, set aside and developed the heavenly abode in the pure positive worlds of God for those who choose to reside there.

Mankind today is trying to make everyone be the same and it is impossible for all of us to be in the same heaven, for we all do not think nor have the same understanding.

We have to develop ourselves individually and think for ourselves, not letting others do our thinking for us. You should decide what you want to do and where you are going and how you are going to get there without others making that decision for you. Each step of the way, including initiations, is your choice and should be your choice without anyone else making these decisions for you. Otherwise, it can cause problems.

It is a healthy situation for an individual to be looking beyond himself, trying to do things he has not done before, being investigative, being bold and adventuresome, because experience is the only way you can gain wisdom. Somebody else cannot give it to you. You can be led through the initiations and the spiritual exercises into circumstances that will give you some wisdom, but you have to learn to live life and know what life is all about.

We must be active in the stream of life. We cannot set ourselves aside from the rest of the world. Let those who think they have religion or some spiritual insight, think this. But the initiate, by living the life of spirit and subtly showing that he has something others do not have, an inner joy, peace and happiness, may have to stand his ground, for others may try to wipe that smile off. By standing his ground through his knowledge of the principles of spirit, greater insights into the mysteries of God are gained.

The teachings are for all people in all worlds and it has always been so, regardless of what planet they were on or what language they spoke.

It is a universal language which is spoken of as music, the Bani which rides upon the sound current. Spirit, the vehicle of God, or the essence of God, whatever one wishes to call it, or spirit itself, is only a training ground for soul for experience here on Earth. And if the individual isn't having any experiences, he can ask the inner master why, then let go and go on to other pursuits, knowing that when the individual is spiritually ready, the experience will come. By letting go and not letting the mind continually bring it up in front of you, you will have it. But be prepared, for some of the experiences are very, very subtle, and you won't realize them until after they have happened.

Many miss what takes place during the few minutes the initiation is given. The master is not there in his physical body, but he is there in the light body, as well as one or two of the ancient masters, just as during a discussion class.

The teacher is never alone, let alone the student. Anytime two or three gather together in a class, they have one of the masters of this ancient order from the invisible realm. There has been a rule set up for discipline and that is that the study class needs to be registered with the initiator of your city or state for spiritual protection established by this ancient order of the masters.

Many prefer to study by themselves and they should not be pushed into attending classes. They wish to study alone because they are at a different level of consciousness, and when they see that the class is gaining and those in it sometimes unfolding swifter, they might visit and take a look, but it is their choice, and that's the way it should be. They will have outflow eventually for no one can keep this spirit bottled up inside for long.

As one unfolds more and awakens, one learns that as an Initiate we cannot wish someone something-- whether it is love, a healing, even good will, for we are setting up conditions for another person. As each Initiate takes on more responsibility, we treat our fellow man with a detached love, talking out differences unemotionally with good will.

When people are unable to talk things out in this fashion they have not gotten beyond the astral plane, let alone the mental plane. If something needs to be handled, it is our responsibility to see about handling it rather than have it eat away within us or becoming passive. This should be true in a family, at school or at work.

Voicing one's opinion when it is strongly felt in that balance of truth can cost one his job, as has happened to me and to others I've known at times, but no one can take away anything in the outer.

We still have something that is greater than anything physical or material that anyone can throw in front of us. We work with people, not controlling them, but have them carry out responsibilities in their function, but always by turning loose of our emotional feelings and not being attached to any status of our life.

Remember, the only thing you can take to heaven is the spiritual knowledge you learn here.

If Spirit sets into motion certain things to take place for us, let it happen. We are to learn to let go of the emotional and intellectual side of ourselves, maintaining our independence and individuality, while allowing spirit to guide us spiritually via the inner master. This factor of responsibility is important to us all over the world as individuals only. It is no one's business but our own.

One should not be passive in one's ways. Take part in life the way you want to take part in it. Whether it is your occupation or what you want to do in expressing spirit, the Holy Ghost, or that which is the essence that is expressed through us, the essence of God.

The one thing that you will find very rewarding and uplifting, is to be detached; being a vehicle for God, letting it flow out and reach out to those that need help, that are asking for it. In this way you start to become a co-worker with God, you do not have to even see or know who will receive the help.

Sometimes a petition is made through prayer by others, meditation, or someone seeking God-enlightenment, but you will find that the fewer petitions made, the more adventuresome one becomes. And this is what it is about.

To be bold and adventuresome, not really looking to some big events that are going to happen or some big experience, but enjoying the moment of this day. This is the uniqueness of that succor that is available. But you have to take a little initiative upon yourself. That is your responsibility.

Man cannot hurt himself if he hangs onto that current because within soul, there is no way it can be aberrated or hurt. It is up to us to break the patterns that we have let others form for us, whether they stem from a past life or from this present life. This is one reason why the masters do not allow those who give talks to become emotional. One should not try to change another's life, because the step must be theirs to take. You are going to come to know yourself to a greater extent and start to love that part of you which is a part of God.

Out of body travel deals with movements of the lesser bodies in the lower worlds only. That which concerns total awareness has nothing to do with the lower worlds. It deals with the soul plane, level or dimension, and beyond to the true abode of God. Upon traveling from the physical to the astral, dropping the astral body and going to the mental world, learning how to drop that body, you come to the soul body and develop that to its fullest. Then you are turned loose, once you have had the complete training by the masters who have initiated you.

I've found in my study of man here on Earth that very few are ready for initiations into the ancient order of the masters, that the many teachers of the past, of the West and especially of the East, make little distinction as to who has reached a climax of spiritual growth and is truly ready for initiation. From what I have observed in my study it seems that the respective spiritual works or the teaching of these leaders comes second.

Man has placed a social hook on the initiation. It's little more than joining an orthodox religion or cult with some sort of ritual. It's not what it will do for you, but what you do with the initiation that counts spiritually.

In the past and present, one of our greatest obstacles

lies in the fact that many teachings want those interested in their respective works to be initiated at once.

Ninety-nine times out of one-hundred, such an initiation will do more harm than good for the seeker. The individual will seldom have any experience in the spiritual let alone the esoteric realms, and lack of the necessary knowledge of what is in store in the lower levels of heaven.

On top of that, those who join these occult, esoteric and religious groups become dependent upon the teacher or leader rather than learning what they can do for themselves.

Many feel that leaving their teacher or church would cause spiritual damage. What they do not know is that they are truly on their own, and that the various groups and the church want to control the masses.

Look at the Far Right Christian movement, the Moonies, the Kremlin, or the efforts to make the United States a Christian state. Would you want this?

A young man wrote me recently saying he was back in jail, this time with a life sentence, and added: "Once again this was beyond my control, I had nothing to do with any of it."

He is failing to see that no one put him behind bars but himself. The master does not interfere with the law of man or spirit. That young man is reaping exactly what he has put out in attitude and behavior. He is indeed, or can be, in control of his life, but as many do, he finds it easier to believe that he is like the leaf in the wind, blown here and there, unaccountable for the events in his life, which is not true.

When we come into areas of awareness that we are unable to write about, it can only be touched upon and expressed through poetry, music, and the arts. It is a polarization that takes place, the polarizing and balancing of the love within us as individuals.

If we try to capture and hold that spirit within ourselves and bottle it up, it will explode. It can cause physical problems and damage to the body. It is like carrying around TNT or nitroglycerin, and as you know, the spirit has to be handled carefully, gently, given out and let go in order for you to receive more of it, for it is the law unto itself and must be obeyed.

The spirit is far greater than TNT or the hydrogen bomb. Once the polarization and the balancing within us, and within the physical structure as well as the soul body takes place, the changes that occur are always for the better of the individual and his spiritual growth.

Without the experience or the knowingness that comes with experience, there is no other way during one's lifetime in which he or she can know.

Many get hung up and stop, either in the mental worlds or the universal worlds, or the soul plane.

From day to day, and moment to moment, each moment of each day is not the same, and there is going to be some ups and downs, because it is not easy here. I'd be suspicious of those who say it is.

Only the individual can find some degree of peace while he is here on this physical plane of existence, within himself. That temple within is only the starting point for the initiate:

1) to become acquainted with himself,
2) have some degree of self-realization,

and 3) learn how to come and go from this temple, not to Europe, or South America, but to the Wisdom Temples and ultimately above time, space, and matter, beyond the soul plane into the God-conscious state.

Some of you may experience it on the way home tonight, or in a week or two, or six months from now. But it's there, so do not be frightened or shaken.

I know when I experienced, objectively, going beyond the physical plane for the first time, I shook for days, however very happy. Unless you are prepared, it is frightening to the physical senses and to the mind. I didn't want to stay home. I wanted to run out into the countryside, and I did. I couldn't find any peace or quietness, because you cannot escape it. Once it chooses us, our whole worlds are shaken depending on the karma we have built up, and we have that opportunity to look back later and say, "I have come a long way, yet there is a long way to go." It all depends on our attitude how we progress as we grow spiritually.

This divine spirit, which is love, may not be for all people even though it sustains all life. We try to give it to those whom we think might be ready for more. They are radiant with the understanding they have gained, whether it is through some philosophy or through life itself. But you and I must be careful, for that person may not be ready. We have to ask ourselves, "Did he ask a question? Is he opening up the door for me to tell him a little more?" If you can just guide him to a book or to a tape or a talk, your job is finished. You then become detached from that person without deciding or trying to make up that person's mind for him.

We don't want the initiates winding up in hospitals or

88

with hypertension or in a neurotic state. We want to keep your feet on the ground. It is all right to have your heart in heaven, but you want to keep your feet on the ground.

This is the reason for unfolding slowly, so that when you are ready for the next step and take it, not only can y ou handle it and unfold into that area of greater or finer vibration, but it is one you will find is gentler than the wind or a buttercup.

To ride out on the sound current with the light that one sees within himself is contact with the body of the master, and if you realize that that is flowing through you during your contemplative exercises, that something is being given to you, and at the same time as it leaves, it is taking out an old trait or habit, an old way of thought, the teachings unfold you consciously into an awareness your mind can grasp. Nothing is taken away without replacing it with something greater.

Beginning before the early days of the history books, and the old teachers of the scriptures, until 1965, it took that span of time before man or a greater number of individuals within the masses, were ready for it, a greater step in consciousness. Man will destroy Earth and himself unless he rids the Earth of his atomic weapons. It is not a prophecy that I am making, but it is one of the reasons for the need for positive vehicles to be co-workers with God, not only on the physical plane of existence, but on the astral, causal, mental, and the soul plane. For the teachers and saints who assist with the running of the universe work with the lesser currents, and when you meet the master, Yaubl Sacabi, you will understand what I am saying.

The Spirit is the most powerful source in this world and in all of the heavenly planes of God. It is a force that is invisible. Also, we find that the greatest source in man is that which is invisible. For the divine power, or love, is that side of man that should always be moving into the higher and greater awareness of God.

The only way in which spirit can manifest itself is through the process of thinking. Thinking is not the only vehicle God can use to aid or hinder mankind, and thought is the only product of thinking. This, of course, pertains to the physical worlds and to man's positive force or for Kal (Satan), the negative force.

Bearing this in mind, additions and subtractions are spiritual transactions; the reasoning of this God source is a spiritual process. Ideas are conceptions through which we are able to be of a positive nature for spirit.

Questions are spiritual searchings, and logic, argument and philosophy are spiritual machinery as long as the individual keeps them out of the area of emotions.

If the spiritual process works through the thinking faculty, the power of this motor is the feeling process. In mechanical terms, the motor is the mind, but the fuel is the heart or subconscious power induced by spirit. One cannot operate without one or the other to any degree at all and have any measure of success in the spiritual worlds or here on Earth, unless one uses force and steps on or dominates people that get in their way.

Thus, every thought combined with feeling brings into action certain physical tissue parts of the brain, the nerves, and including the muscles. This introduces actual change in the condition of the tissue regardless of whatever body it may be - physical, causal or mental.

Therefore, it is only necessary to have certain thoughts combined with feeling on a given idea such as love, in order to bring about a complete change in the organization of man through the Spirit.

Chapter 6

THE HOLY AFFAIR

The fellow man on the street, regardless of what country he is from, watches the initiate because of that succor he has, that substance flowing through that is spirit. People see and feel it. It is through the initiations that you receive a greater amount of that, providing you know how to work with it, to laugh at yourself and at someone else who might, not necessarily poke fun at you, but while not meaning to test you, accidentally "push the button" to move you emotionally, then let go.

When I first heard this term, "pushing someone's buttons," at some of the early seminars and among gatherings, I wondered what that meant, so I stayed off to the side, looked and listened, and in doing so, I recognized what they meant by "pushing the button." What one is doing is creating a karmatic bond that sooner or later must be worked out.

Some of these button-pushers would see someone who might be new to the teachings, or who had been in a few years, and would say something that would upset that person emotionally. That person would walk away grumbling and become irritable with others, while the button-pusher filled himself full of love and let it flow out. But it can boomerang and be like pulling the rug out from under one. We can joke with each other and have fun, for I enjoy a laugh, but every action has an equal and opposite reaction.

Occasionally, Rebazar Tarzs, (the Master in charge of the teachings here on Earth, who lives in the Hindu Kush Mountains), and Paul Twitchell and I get together and laugh quite frequently. However, when it comes to guiding the individual in his spiritual self (Soul), that part of you that the masters guide spiritually through the lower worlds, no one will ever poke fun at you. We might be out here with you constantly and you may not see us, for you are never alone, but we won't trick you, and when we do have a laugh, whether it's on the outer or in the dream state, we'll be face to face.

There are charlatans, entities who like to poke fun at people in the lower worlds. And this we know. There are some that even try to appear as Rebazar Tarzs or Peddar Zaskq or myself or one of the other masters, but if you are not sure, don't be afraid to challenge them. Especially if someone is poking fun at you, terrifying you, or having you do or say something you feel uncomfortable about, call on the Mahanta. The true Masters don't do that.

I've told before about the experience I had one time with Paul. One evening while I was contemplating, doing my spiritual exercises, trying to expand my awareness on a particular subject, I found myself in a scene with Paul. I was beyond myself and had projected myself to a spot where Paul was with three or four people, at a sidewalk cafe of sorts having tea. All at once I was in their midst. Suddenly he turned around, looked me squarely in the eye, put a big cigar in his mouth and puffed on it, looking at me as if to say, "Now, what do you want?" You can imagine my shock! He had allowed me to come into his presence for that moment of time and I didn't ask questions, for it was a test, nor did I go around saying Paul Twitchell smoked cigars. You see most of us have been taught to think that a cigar is a no-no and we jump to conclusions.

It was a funny scene to me later after I really thought about it. I laughed at it for I couldn't get angry with him. I was being tested and if I'd gotten angry I would have slipped backwards spiritually. He had allowed me to come into his presence, in soul, to where he was. You move in soul and it doesn't take place on this physical plane of existence. It took place elsewhere and he set it up for me. The masters are very clever, beautiful and full of love. You are unable to out-do them. I didn't look upon this act as a practical joke, but as a lesson. I had a few things to learn and it helped round me out a bit, polished a few areas that were rough in my thinking, how I looked at things when I saw them, and helped me not to judge by my first impression of what I see happening to or with another person.

This is something each of us must have some degree of control within ourselves, including Trust, Ethics, Integrity and being Honest, as well as being Conscientious about all that we say and do, at home, work, etc.

We see some funny things sometimes and set up very strange images, mental images. It's not easy to control them but we can laugh at them, without judging immediately, and step aside and look at the experience, back away from it, just as I did. I was immediately ready to judge Paul Twitchell, then caught myself, for who am I to judge somebody else?

I pondered and slept on it for a couple of days, because I was in training at that time just as each of us are for mastership of our own world. When I really got a good look at it after contemplation, I started laughing and couldn't stop. There is an old saying that if you laugh too much, or a whole lot, it puts weight on you, and I wondered then if Buddha had laughed a bunch!

I gained a fair understanding of the teachings that say one must walk the middle path, neither being for nor against anything and recognizing his fellow human being, accepting each for what he is, not putting him down for what he might say or what he might do.

In our daily life out in the world, we have to interact with whomever we come in contact with in a certain way. This whole world is a stage and the people you meet in life are the playwrights, as well as the audience and the directors, for you are a reflection in their eyes.

You have to act and put on that intellectual mask and use the same words and phrases as those people you deal with on a day-to-day basis.

It is different, however, among fellow initiates. You have to be very straightforward, very sincere and honest, and if you aren't being honest with yourself and your fellow man, you are not being honest with God. You then are only kidding yourself. You are then pushing against that inner door and it is not going to open, no matter how hard you try or what you do.

Who are you trying to impress anyway? Surely not spirit nor God. IT knows even your thoughts before you think them, not to speak of your actions.

In your day-to-day living here and now, be yourself, above all. Be as aware as you can of what you do, what physical and mental gestures are made. How you look helps to get you along in this world of existence. You have to get out here in a state of consciousness and look at yourself. This can be developed but you will reach God quicker than you think, if the attitude is right.

When you move beyond yourself in awareness, you may hear a little click and find you've gone subjectively or objectively out in your soul body. Many do not recognize or realize when this is taking place. But when you are startled into returning to the physical realm again, stop and think: "Where was I before?"

One time a young man wrote me that when he contemplated, all he ever got in the way of experience was a slight click sound, nothing else. Another chela mentioned that all she ever saw in contemplation was "a blue light." They both were expecting more than they understood, but what they will realize someday is that both the click and the blue light are evidences of having gone beyond their state of consciousness of awareness in the presence of the inner master. And this realization is a very precious, sacred thing, for they have been well blest.

During a walk recently, I spotted a young man stretched out on a lawn with his camera, the lens trained on a squirrel. The squirrel was obviously intent upon the cameraman, scampering this way and that, running around, not looking at anyone else but straight into the camera.

The squirrel was a little ham and he knew it. I knew it too. It's the little things around us that give us pleasure and a few special moments of the holy affair we have with spirit, like when we sing a song, whistle to ourselves and laugh with family and friends, or at things and people around us. As I mentioned in an earlier chapter, humor is an aspect of the survival factor. It is often the very thin line between life and death, sanity and insanity.

There are many great spiritual travelers and spiritual giants that do exist and do their work from greater planes of existence known as Sat Lok, that plane of being where there is no form as we know form, which is the first manifestation of what we call God or the Sugmad, the one God of many. It is a pure positive God world.

Out of this world issues energy with a vibratory rate coming down through each and every plane of the lower worlds. It sustains all life as you know it and is known as spirit. It is not God Itself. The orientals call this energy "Prana," and each individual who laughs and smiles manifests this energy. It is also what you inhale into your lungs, and then let out. It is what man calls electricity, but as electricity it is of a much lesser form, yet much greater than that which we get from a generator.

This energy that sustains us as human beings, this divine spirit, it is received in a vibratory rate and can be seen as Light and heard as Sound. It rides through the cosmic sea, through each and every plane of existence and on to give life which sustains the material worlds and universes.

This rate of frequency that human beings exist upon is a so-called Prana. It is Spirit known down through time. Some have more flowing through them than others, for it can be seen in many ways. It is the life force and those who have a greater amount will be more creative, yet another person with the same amount may not show it in ways we think of as creativity. Then there are those who are on the low end of life's survival scale and have little or no initiative, and in most cases become a burden upon their families or society as a whole.

In the foundation of the sciences, spirit is there. Man is confronted with just a small portion of what he calls energy, yet once one learns of the totality of God, he does not want to have anything to do with the rest of the universe. However, he won't take his life because of this knowledge.

The great spiritual masters that have chosen to retain their bodies here are doing so purposely to help the Living Master and those individual souls who wish to gain spiritual freedom of all things in life, have complete independence and freedom from the materialistic world.

There are those in the past that have ridiculed the teachings and the inner master. They will learn or have learned through experience that to hold any overt or covert act against spirit or anyone high in the spiritual life, is only doing themselves a wrong because it reflects back to that person.

It is a vibration that is not sent out by the individual ridiculed, but from spirit itself. That overt or covert thought produces a vibratory rate that rides out between the two individuals and is received. But that thought, feeling or action returns it to the sender.

The ethics of the initiate should be of the highest nature that man will ever know on this planet from this teaching, much higher than is known by the masses of the world. However, a word of caution here: Some who may have the initiations may not have unfolded spiritually and may have no ethics or very few.

The love that is written about and spoken of is a higher divine love which does issue out of the pure positive God worlds, but that love sustains all life, acts as a catalyst and binding force and is a part of the spirit itself. If misused by one who knows how to be a vehicle for IT against another, used other than for that person's own good, the user must pay for it. This is a law of Spirit.

To understand the audible life stream, which is not easy at first, requires developing yourself in steps of vibratory rates so as to understand yourself greater as a human being. It takes a little action on your part, not becoming passive. Meditation leads to a passive state and those who are initiated will find they cannot become passive.

Contemplation allows you to sit in silence while developing some action or the understanding of a subject within yourself, this world or the heavenly worlds.

Thoughts which produce some of these vibratory rates are sent out as forms which ultimately must manifest, and the sender must be responsible for these thought forms.

We do not pray for the divine to give us something as individuals. Instead, we ask for that, in a positive manner, which would benefit all in our receiving.

By so doing we are lifting ourselves above the level of self-involving thought and giving greater significance to helping ourselves by doing for others.

This is what the masses do not understand nor something the religious orders want their followers to know about. Jesus, God, Buddha or Mohammed will not hear their cries for they turn a deaf ear to this world.

Remember, until you understand that nothing can happen to you, nothing can ever come to you or be kept away from you except in accordance with the state of your consciousness, you do not have the key to life.

Man tends to confine his efforts to the lower worlds, rarely going beyond the mental plane of existence. But when you get to the place where you can rise above the lower worlds and see from the whole, you can have the true bliss which no man on the face of this Earth can tell you about.

This is the soul plane or Sat Lok, the first plane of existence, once man has passed through the lower worlds. He is guided through the lower worlds to his true home by the master, if he chooses this, and if he has earned this opportunity in this lifetime.

Getting into the soul plane is not easy but the fruits of the teachings, as Paul Twitchell stated in his writings are peace, joy, health, love and prosperity. Not a car or a mansion on the hill, but a prosperity far beyond the mind and the human conception of the mental realm.

Yet there is health, peace, bliss, and prosperity that comes with this entry once you reach the fifth plane and go beyond, because ultimately you get to that point when you drop everything, all attachments, inside and outside. Yet some misunderstand that they still are to maintain their responsibilities in this physical universe. You learn you do not have to give up your personal items. We don't just go off into the hills and contemplate our navels. You start taking hold of all life and being responsible for every action and vibratory note set forth. You come to understand that with every breath you draw and every flower you see and every smile that is witnessed with the optical part of yourself, you are seeing spirit. This is part of the holy affair.

But greater is that which is better known as spirit in the light form. There, in that particular dimension, is a vibratory rate that can lift you above good and evil. When you reach that point of knowingness you are above karma. Those on the path of the ancient teachings reach the higher initiations and drop everything in the inner and outer planes. Then you understand what it really means not to put down another person or living thing. When a child cries or is disciplined by a parent in a store or in a park, you feel the vibrations and it upsets you. It's not easy to say you'll let go of it and let happen what happens. There are times it's very difficult to control the emotions that are induced by various actions of vibratory rates.

Many of the saints had the ability to utilize the cosmic current to help those who were seeking higher spiritual understanding. They were doing great things in their own way. Humility, along with love, can lead you, if you take it to the inner master, to where you start to unfold and understand yourself as a human being, the world that you live in and the higher worlds. This produces a certain frequency within the individual and radiates out in this vibratory rate, and what goes forth must be returned. For it flows away with that which issues out of Sugmad from the center within the heart of God. In that way, when it has reached the outer limits it returns to the center.

The way to truth is simple, yet difficult, for the way to know God is to know one's self, and to face one's self in one's own consciousness. To face truth is to realize that life is one in and through its manifestations. To have this understanding is to forget the limited life in the realization of the unity of life on all planes of God.

The lie is greater than truth in the worlds of kal, and no truth is greater than the lie, and truth is never greater than no truth for one must be guided by love and truth to reach into the heart of God.

The spiritual travelers, the silent ones (who are far greater than the spiritual travelers) are there to help assist those souls who have been longing to get back to what they have been told is home, and which is home, from where they have originated as soul and were sent forth to the lower worlds for experience. This is all we are here for, to gain the spiritual experience of being.

When you force your impressions on another individual and he isn't ready to receive them, this sets up an inner emotion within yourself in a different vibratory rate of negative polarization.

If it is sent out, if you inwardly hang onto it and let the mind chew on it and let it get lodged within the consciousness, it builds greater waves until you think sometimes that all heaven and hell have come tumbling down around you.

These are experiences that are necessary for some

individuals because they don't have the understanding to let go and become detached from certain emotions. These emotions, both positive and negative, set up certain vibratory rates. Inward peace is not truth. When you take life as it comes once you reach the higher planes, you gain and know that you are working with the Sugmad because you become very careful not only of the steps you take, the thoughts you think, but of the words you say.

Spirit of Itself does not manifest within things although all things are manifested by the light and sound of God. However, all material things do have their own vibratory rate or aura. You can feel vibrations as you walk down the street, and you are not becoming sensitive, you are becoming aware. A sensitive person is working off the astral plane. We do not use the physical, astral, causal, mental or etheric bodies, we use the soul body.

The Mahanta, the Living Master will head you in the right direction if you choose this, but he will not take the steps for you, you must ask. This is why the teachings are for the individual. It is up to you to have this holy affair with the Supreme Being, at your own pace and time. All souls will, eventually.

Only within the soul body is there perfection. As Man is trying to seek perfection here on the physical plane, trying to draw God, or his ruler, down to his level of understanding, the question is raised: "Who created God?"

Man actually did in his own thoughts. In the early Christian days, Man had to see things happen with his physical eyes. He had to see the heavens open up, and the angels from the astral and the causal plane, in order to understand that there is something beyond this physical plane of existence.

Long before Christianity was started, the concepts of great teachers were put down because they were telling the truth. Some of these concepts may have evolved here on Earth. Those who are arguing and getting all emotional about this creation business forget that all the bibles, holy books and other records down through time have written about men in machines coming out of the skies or heavens, landing, eating, talking and even partaking of the local women. I know they have also seeded this world from distant universes.

So hear ye! Not all of us who are here on Earth came up from the sea, animals or bird kingdom. Some of us have come from other universes, galaxies and planets which support life as we know it. I know that there are people of different colors on some of the planets. This is something you can prove to yourself through a spiritual exercise called the easy way as spelled out in my other writings.

All through man's history, each and every one that has given out a little bit of truth to mankind has been ridiculed. While developing ourselves as human beings we must keep in mind the importance of attitude. The attitudes of most saints were those of devotion and love; however, not all of them had these attitudes. Many put on a good front and when the people's backs were turned, their doings would put Al Capone to shame.

The attributes of the Mahanta, the Living Master, and

the spiritual travelers and what has been written in the wisdom temples on the planes of God are truth. I doubted that the set of books existed on these planes, yet I had the feeling they might. I'm referring to books called The Way of the Eternal. They are there and I have seen and read them. When I visited the temple on the astral plane with Gopal Das, the Master who is in charge of that temple, I became a believer. Seeing and reading is believing.

Explaining the astral plane and experiencing it are two different things. The entities there are very much like the ones here in form, but the colors are more brilliant at the highest level. On the lower levels they are gray or black and white. There are a great number of individuals there whom you read about in history books. There are also great ministers from this plane, and some are trying to get beyond the astral realm because they have heard of this path. This is only due to the work of Paul Twitchell, who is also known spiritually as Peddar Zaskq.

Being brave, adventuresome and bold, he took upon his shoulders the responsibility of bringing the truth and teachings out into the worlds at this time in history. He had to study every teaching on Earth and even join some to learn how they functioned for he did not wish to make some of their mistakes. It was part of his training.

His book, The Far Country, existed in the libraries on the astral plane before it came out on this plane of existence. In spreading the word of God on these lower planes, the astral, causal and mental, the same kind of problems exist there as here because of the teachings that have been set up throughout history.

Paul never had to plagiarize anyone's books as some have tried to accuse him. He had access to material on the heavenly planes that the masters helped him bring into publication on this Earth plane. There is much that Man does not understand about the spiritual giants, but he will try to disqualify and annihilate the efforts of the vehicle for the Sugmad rather than believe that such a Being exists.

On the planet Venus is another Master, Rami Nuri, and there are some who have developed themselves to move beyond Venus and can visit the spiritual city of Agam Des. The Beings on Venus are more evolved than the Beings on this planet, yet they have similar problems as we do. We have an opportunity not only to become a co-worker but to see things beyond verbal description that does not exist in our libraries nor in the greatest dictionaries that you can find in our libraries.

There is a library on the astral plane where one who has earned the right can obtain wisdom and knowledge not found anywhere else. They earn this right through development, study, labors, by expanding their consciousness, but they have to do it themselves. One learns to keep the proper attitude at a particular level, not to be for nor against anything, yet to have one's opinion. As one climbs the spiritual ladder, he obtains a secret initiation word all his own and works off his karma while still existing in the physical body.

You will know and understand when you start heading downward in a state of consciousness whether you incurred this from meeting someone on the street, or walking through a building and picking it up or just from a thought form that issued out of yourself. Some of these litttle traits are from past lives. This is where the master can help you from the invisible side of life. What he will do is set you in the right direction, yet it will be up to you to carry it out yourself.

Those who read auras and attempt to heal through what they call "cleansing of the aura" are taking on problems of that individual rather than helping him. When it is a trait from a past life, another cannot clean it out for you. The master will guide you and point you in the right direction but he will not do it for you. Telling others how they feel or what they should or should not do without their permission is a violation of the spiritual law. That is true of prayer also. Praying for others without their explicit permission is a violation of the spiritual law and of their psychic space. Have you noticed that where there is a huge religious push for some program, such as wiping out some activity believed to be negative, a greater negative thing appears? They do not see this or are ignorant of it.

One must develop himself to become a master because what is latent within the human being is and has been given to each and every individual; however, after you reach a certain place on the spiritual ladder of life, you will need assistance to go farther into the heavenly worlds or that known as the Kingdom of Heaven.

Even the Jesuits are limited and work from the etheric plane of heaven which is the subconscious part of us as human beings. Let me tell you, they have done some very negative things to the masses and individuals in the past. The Lords of Karma will be rectifying this.

The vibratory rate is an energy spoken of as the Audible Life Stream and is issued out through the one God, Sugmad, the one God of all gods, including the negative force.

I met a man at a seminar one time who asked me what I'd been drinking for he had seen me going around to people, smiling, shaking hands, very happy and nothing upsetting me, and I told him I wasn't drinking anything--physical, that is.

What happens on the inner planes I try not to show too much on the outer, but that nectar, that wine of God, called Kaloma Nod, is not just for one or two people, it is for everyone if they make the effort to work for it and find it. This is what the spiritual travelers and the Living Master can do for the chela.

Chapter 7

ONE'S LIFE WORK

I am often asked by the people of this world to help them decide what avocation to follow, what job opportunity to try for, what professional area to get into. I usually answer: "What do you want to do? What do you like to do?"

Paul Twitchell used to tell of discussing personal situations with chelas and advising them of what course to take, only to have them do the exact opposite. He would marvel that they had asked his advice in the first place.

The duty and responsibilities of the master cover the individual's spiritual life here and in the heavenly worlds when asked. It is up to the individual to take care of his physical life in the way best suited for him.

Music and art forms are a very important part of life. Some are capable of making these areas their life's work, others are not so fortunate. They may have a talent or skill in artistic measures, but not enough training or ability to earn a living from it. Sometimes the master will work with these individuals on the inner planes to develop their talents so they can make their way in the world, and be vehicles through which spirit can move. Some artists, musicians, painters, and mystics have had some knowledge of obtaining contact with spirit through the masters, yet they knew them as a guardian angel or spiritual guide. One is fortunate to know this, which makes one modest and humble about any success he or she achieves. And by keeping this modesty along with their success, they maintain a balance within their lives. The modesty that one keeps within himself is a form of good karma, for to succeed or not to succeed, as man thinks of success has no bearing in this area.

Music is a wonderful source of enlightenment. I found in the concert tours I have shared with *Darwin & Friends*, wonderful experiences had taken place. Through light and lilting melodies, ballads, light and subtle sounds and happy blues, souls soared to heights never known before. The music served to sweep out old images, set patterns and rigid thinking. Many were totally surprised at a master who played the blues! But why not? It derives from soul.

The world has been beset with harsh sounds such as punk rock, acid rock, loud boisterous vibrations called "music" by individuals who may, unconsciously, not realize what they are setting into motion. Their jarring sounds bring into play the lowest of consciousness, animalistic and ear-puncturing at best, degrading and degenerating at its worst. This type of "music" does not carry healing vibrations of any kind. Its vibrations are designed instead to tear apart cells and break down protein and tissues in the body, a scientific fact!

Each master who spends a tour of responsibility on the Earth planet, and all the galaxies and universes within the realms of Sugmad, has some form of communication he uses to reach the uninitiated. Paul Twitchell was a prolific writer and lecturer, having the great task of bringing the oldest spiritual teaching known to mankind to the waiting modern world. It was a struggle all the way for Paul, as told in a book called Difficulties Of Becoming The Living Master. His background of newspaper journalism and creative writing became a natural and effective way for the masters to bring the message to a seeking and disturbed world.

Thanks to Paul's tenacity and natural skills, the world has a yardstick by which to judge spiritual experiences, accounted for through his writings.

Music has always been a strong factor in my background this lifetime. Even as a small child, I played some instrument, for my family always had musical instruments around to play.

You Can't Turn Back details my life story, the struggle through the youth years, knowing I had a spiritual guide and recognizing him when I saw a picture of Paul Twitchell on his biography by Brad Steiger's, In My Soul I Am Free.

The concert tour that covered Europe, the South Pacific, the United States and Canada in late 1980 and throughout 1981, coupled with autographing sessions of my biography proved to be an astounding experience for all concerned.

Hundreds wrote me they had experienced healings during the concert itself, or they had received inner experiences they had never had before. It was no coincidence that the uplifting and enlightening music presented, ballads and soft happy blues, contained the elements to heal and regenerate thousands who were receptive.

In the selection of songs I have chosen to play or have written, I've always attempted to introduce the therapeutic effects upon the listener or for my own enjoyment. It is a known fact that the beat is the core of the selection of music. I have in most cases attempted to play a slower beat. Why? The tempo faster than the human heartbeat not only excites a more rapid heartbeat, but with the tempo up in most forms of music, the pitch becomes higher and with a greater number of vibrations which produces these sound waves that are very damaging to the core of our selves.

In presenting the softer sounds with a laid back tempo, about the tempo of the human heartbeat, I've been told over the years that my music has been soothing. This is something that is hard to do with electronic music. No matter how it sounds to the ear, it carries a different vibration than does the acoustic instrurment.

With electronic music on the up swing, I find it is difficult to replace music produced by the human hand. I would rather listen to the Sound Current which cannot be reproduced, for it is God's music, the music of the spheres.

Although I had relatively little technical background, I had the good fortune to work with a professional engineer as his project design engineer, learning all I could from him. He was amazed with the innate abilities and knowledge that I could draw upon (from spirit) to get results on problems that baffled the experts.

Electronics were as natural to me as music, which eventually moved me into a job as a magnetic design engineer in the silicon valley.

114

Most of the knowledge I needed with any of the jobs I had came from the ability to get beyond the physical into the higher planes. Inventions flowed through me but were often misunderstood and viewed with suspicion because they were light-years ahead of man's technology.

As stated previously, inventions stem from the astral plane and man has access to their use if they are used for the benefit of mankind, rather than for the purpose of lining one's pockets.

I was never without an opportunity to work if work was what I wanted to do. Many do not use the gifts and skills they have at their fingertips to earn a living for themselves and their families. Common sense and initiative, being bold and adventuresome, tapping into that substance that sustains life, the Divine Spirit-- these are the qualities that allow the individual to broaden his horizon.

A young gentleman who had just learned about this teaching spoke with me about being out of work for some time. He called upon the master to help him get a job and got one the very next day. But the reason this man was given a job was that he took a little effort upon himself, went about filling out applications and then did not worry about the job he was going to be given. He is quite happy making his way in this world.

If man had a different political system and was assured that each and every human being had a chance to make his way so he wouldn't have to worry about feeding himself and his family, he'd be freer to think more about his spiritual growth and development. Yet in the country each of us lives in, we must abide by these laws of that country and nation. Sometimes it is very hard, but know that the spirit supports you, that there is a greater food that can be had through the HU, an ancient name of God.

Fear for one's security is another limiting facet of life. If one can learn to trust the divine guidance, then get off one's "duff" and take a step toward today's challenges, spirit will provide the opportunity for training needed to get ahead in life.

But trust is a very important commodity. That means not sitting around and waiting for life to happen to you.

The state of the individual's health is also a consideration. The chronically ill individual is not inspired to venture forth into life, whether the illness is actual or imagined.

Those who partake of the Audible Life Stream (the Sound Current) find they don't have to eat much, for over-eating is gluttony. It is necessary that one keep a balance in his material life, his outer life. A balance of not only what to eat and drink, and the way you eat or drink it, but of what you say and do as well.

The masters who dwell in the physical realm eat little or nothing. Some drink only tea but their vibrations are very high. Fubbi Quantz, who lives in the Katsupari Monastery in northern Tibet, eats a little fowl, fresh vegetables, a little fuit, drinks tea, and consumes very little cooked foods. Man knows that cooking the food loses many of the minerals. I feel best myself when I eat fresh vegetables, fresh fuits and nuts.

Don't let anyone tell you what to do, for it is your freedom to do what is best for yourself. Many children at dinner time say: "I'm not hungry," and we force food

116

on them anyway. They will get hungry a little later. If they have been playing hard and their body-motor is running real hard, they have no appetite. Let them stay away from the table, don't force food on them. Many times forcing food on children has an effect in their later years or on their health. Why eat if you are not hungry, just because the hands of the clock say a certain hour? If your system isn't ready for food, let it alone.

Sometimes if you are over-eating a particular food you should not be eating, you will be shown in the dream state. I recall one summer in 1967-68, I was eating far too many ice cream cones. One night in the dream state I was handed an ice cream cone by the master and in it was a substance I sure didn't like, it tasted like shit. I stopped eating ice cream cones, for it wasn't good for my chemical structure at that point in time.

If you are shown something of this nature, take the warning, bank on it, learn to trust not only the Dream Master but the inner master or guardian angel working with you. Trust and rely upon this inner master and you'll grow by leaps and bounds. For that love that is a catalyst and a supporting force, not only of this universe but of all worlds of God, supports each and every planet very precisely.

There is a group of some past saints, various holy men that exist on the causal plane, and some masters. Their responsibility is to keep all of the worlds and universes in perfect running order, although within the physical worlds and the lower psychic worlds, nothing is perfect. Man tries to make things perfect, yet this is not possible when there is a negative current.

There can be a balance, but there is nothing perfect here. The only thing that comes near to perfection is the individual's soul body, yet the various sheaths or the electromagnetic field or aura that surrounds and protects the soul body must be purified, and it takes time to purify each body or sheath at a time, one after another, not all at once. You couldn't survive that much power, positive and negative. That much Sound Current would damage the physical body. Yet all heaven and all Earth can fall away today and the initiate knows he/she is taken care of.

We have been taught how to grow old and how to die, but not how to live and stay young. While the physical shell can grow old, the real Self does not grow old. There is no age difference or what man calls the "generation gap." Keep the body healthy and you can have a far greater spiritual experience as you progress in unfoldment while climbing that spiritual ladder of life.

Once the individual gets through the Dark Night of Soul and through that tunnel of Yreka that leads into the soul plane, once the lessons are learned and one goes beyond the soul plane, then the road is not narrow anymore. It is wide and becomes far wider than one's mind can imagine, and far greater. However, remember that on each level of heaven the rules differ.

There is always the opportunity presented to the individual truly wishing to understand more, but not to the masses, although a vast amount of knowledge is available to the masses as well.

As we go along in life, we do not change ourselves. Many will say: "I'm trying to change this or that within myself," whether it is an attitude or whatever, but we should let spirit work with us to do that. The physical world and everything about us is changing constantly, but we do not change. The areas of change that come about within ourselves will let the spirit flow through us. It changes us. We do not change ourselves.

When you start to have problems, sit back and look at yourself from another point of view. View yourself as though you were someone else.

We cause the problem that is within us by trying to change our ways. In this change, whether it concerns a habit or negative trait, or certain words that you use, you will sooner or later expand your consciousness to the point that you will realize that you are letting spirit work with you. It will place you in a postion where you will use those words incorrectly and really embarrass yourself. Then you will tip-toe away for awhile and go off in another direction and pretty soon you will find you have been brought back to the middle path without trying to change yourself.

This is an area where the psychological and medical sciences are unable to help us as individuals. Remember this, when you feel that you are doing something which someone else has set up as a mold for you to fill, ASK the inner master for guidance.

I am asked many times in letters to assist an individual who has gone to the end of his rope with man's ways, with medical knowledge or medicine, and whose situation cannot be corrected whether it is through psychology or voodoo. This is why we have a great deal of conflict in life, in nations and between countries, when trying to change someone else's life, or have others fit a certain mold.

It is the inner communication that can guide you from day to day, moment to moment, in whatever your occupation or endeavors are. Leave the spiritual part to the inner master and try not to change yourself physically, but within; the image of yourself is most important. It ties in with that old saying: "As Above, So Below," using imagination as one of the keys to out of body travel, or moving beyond your present state of awareness.

There is a spiritual exercise used, where you inwardly look obliquely to the right or left, not straight ahead, projecting the image of your goal on the screen of the mind. It is not the thought that moves you into another arena of activity, for the mind should not be controlled. Let it run like a river for otherwise it will hold and bind you to the lower worlds. Place the attention upon soul, the indwelling self. This is the area of survival.

The factor of success lies in using and utilizing the imagination. Imagine yourself where you want to be, in the Wisdom Temple with the Master, or visiting one of the structures on Venus. Don't keep the image always in front of you, but look obliquely to the right or left.

The imagination is there, set it up, and now shift your attention slightly away from the image. At some point in time, after some practice, you will notice a "click" and realize that you have been at the place of your goal. But don't set things into motion without knowing what the outcome is going to be.

It is like the law of reversed effort where we put a plank across an area that is three inches off the ground and have no trouble walking across the plank. But move the plank up in the same area anywhere from five feet to twenty feet high, and we are scared to go across. We have to shore it up to make it solid and we still are afraid to walk across that plank. Sometimes you can back across that plank, look at it a little differently and don't look down, look straight ahead. You want to reach this point from over here to over there and once that imaginative factor has been set into motion, go on to the image of it. This image is the important part. See yourself arriving on the other side of the plank, not falling off the plank and landing on the ground. It is the river-running mind that will cause the fears of falling.

Just using this exercise as a practice will help one to see that he controls his own destiny. Even if the fear takes over and in imagination you fall, instead of plunging downward, fly!

Most of us have seen the ring around the sun or the moon. It is a unit of energy that can be utilized for Man if he understands the image factor, because that ring is just the image from its source or essence transmitting down to Earth, and you and I. We are the image of IT, of God, or Sugmad. However, we are the image of God in Soul, not the physical body as many around the world think.

Once being unmanifested, souls are manifested. We never become less. We do not evolve, we awaken to greater spiritual beings but not in the sense most men think of.

You will find the masters in the Wisdom Temples or on one of the other planes are superhuman beings but very humble.

Do not put them above yourself or the next fellow, and don't be surprised if you meet one once in awhile who is doing a lonely little job or function. You may even wonder: "Was he a master, doing that lowly job with all his knowledge?"

One can be happy at doing almost anything with the proper attitude. That is a factor most of us tend to ignore in the human state of consciousness. Many of the people I worked with harbored a sour or unhappy attitude, holding onto it or becoming involved with another's situation, which upset their emotional or astral body. When they were unhappy and I would sing or whistle, they sometimes would ask me to leave the area or go work somewhere else, but for me, the happy attitude was a state of survival.

We make problems that exist from day to day and set those conditions up for ourselves or let others set them up for us. This is an area one wants to start unfolding in, to control and set up conditions for one's own life. There is good and bad karma, and that guilt factor of sin that is used in the world is a means of control. There is no sin in this teaching; we make our own difficulties or they are impressed upon us by others.

Whenever someone goes too far to the right or the left, by doing everything in the name of the Sugmad or the Mahanta, they will find they will come back to the middle path, the balanced position for happier living. You should always remember to know what the end result is going to be before you go into an experience, but try and have a little fun while you are doing it.

This is a spiritual freedom that the initiates are enjoying. As one starts to unfold into another new area, after a few bouncings back and forth from right to left, they realize that although they are completely free, there are factors that must be considered. Individually as one unfolds, he becomes a greater channel for spirit which is God's vehicle to work with life forms. One cannot help but become a greater channel with a little initiative taken upon oneself and the responsibility to love oneself and God. As this is understood, then one becomes a lover of all life.

Try not to judge your fellow man. If you feel strongly about an issue, stand up and be counted by stating your opinion, but live and let live! You can only know what is right for yourself, no one else. Take the time to evaluate the type of work you want to get into, and if obstacles seem to be standing in your way, get above them with an overview and see what might be holding you back from accomplishing what you wish to accomplish. Or put into writing your feelings, your frustrations, and then let go of them. Put the note in a dresser drawer or tear it up. Just writing it down releases it for spirit to work with you, if you will let go and let spirit handle it. Go on from there.

I've filled out more than fifty applications once and interfered each time with spirit upon looking at what I was doing. I continued but then let go. I went to work very soon after that.

The image of yourself that you act out is very important. How do you feel about yourself? Are you too timid, do you feel "unworthy" to go too far up in a certain line of work or aspiration?

Are you too aggressive, too outgoing so that people are turned off? Think in terms of the middle path, the middle ground. What is the image you would really like to see in yourself, as others observe you? Use this image in practice of the imaginative technique discussed earlier. But then let go of it. Place before yourself the image of your goals and release it so spirit can bring it about, if it is for your benefit and for the good of the whole.

In order to receive anything, one has to give in some manner, even in attitude. The individuals who have a long list of reasons why something won't work rarely believe that their problems stem from within themselves. They will blame someone else, and may never learn that only when they change their attitude towards themselves and others around them, will a greater light enter their lives. Some people apparently prefer to stand in the shadows and complain, instead of coming out into the sunlight and being as Soul.

Do you love yourself enough to bring out the Soul qualities you have within you? Soul is a happy entity and shines like the sun. Remember, It is also lazy, you must push It yourself. When you look at the mirror of life, don't spend time gazing at it. Walk through it, go beyond it and develop that 360-degree viewpoint without judging or setting up conditions for others. See yourself as the Master sees you, not as the mind would have you believe you are.

Chapter 8

LIVE AND LET LIVE!

I am constantly at battle within the lower worlds as well as on this physical plane of being with the two powers known as positive and negative. Many times assisting a chela asking for help on this path, and sometimes not; when the chela doesn't ask, I may still step in to help.

I used to smoke in some of my earlier years, but it dropped away as I developed myself spiritually. There is no emphasis placed on smoking. One should not smoke when they get their second or light and sound Initiation or greater, or they should attempt to drop it. I have never been ill from the smell of smoke; however, in recent years in a commercial airliner, it was very difficult for me to be around cigarette smoke, due to reaching higher and taking on a greater load spiritually. This was hard to understand until this one flight when I experienced smoke in close quarters. However, I sat there and took what came with it, a headache and nausea. Yet I have learned, as many are about to, how to handle these situations.

There are guidelines in life in which to function, since we are in the material physical universe; we need these guidelines, for even the planetary system is very precisely run in a very strict order, but once you get beyond the physical, astral and mental worlds, you will find that the rules and regulations are very different on each plane or level of heaven, and when you return into this human state of consciousness, you will find there is a factor that is needed to reach into the pure positive God worlds. It is a factor that a great deal of us tend to forget from day to day, sometimes from moment to moment, one which isn't easy to keep in mind out there in the world when there is a lot of negative force attempting to pull us down and hold us back. Sometimes this is set up by another person's thoughts or thought patterns about us, and whether they are fellow initiates makes no difference.

This one factor I am referring to is love of the master, or you can think of it as love of God. You will find that the master is the vehicle, not the physical part, but in the radiant body, and if you can think of it as the love of the Mahanta, or inter master, or that presence that is always with the initiate, with those who recognize it, it is a factor of love far greater than most have heard of. It is not that physical love that is only a temporary and momentary thing, at the low end of the totem pole.

At the high end is that expression that is beyond words, which the musician, the composer or dancer, the poet, the writer, attempts to portray through his works. This higher love can only be shared, this feeling for life and others, by turning it over to spirit, or the Mahanta, the inter master, to share with others. If you have that factor of doing everything in the name of the Sugmad, or the Mahanta, it is another vibration and there is nothing that you will do without it when you become accustomed to it. With everything that you do, and regardless of what walk of life you tread or whether you are doing anything at all, from one morning to the next, your day is going to go greater.

You can be in the wildest forest or wildest jungle, or a riot can be happening around you on the streets, and you will not be affected. You go about your way and remove yourself from that atmosphere unharmed. It comes with practicing the presence of God, or the presence of the Mahanta, but more than that, when you are filled with love for life, the negative cannot resist that love and it must step aside.

IT of itself longs to have each and every Soul back in ITs own domain, but on the path you yourself choose whether you become one with God, an atom in an atom structure, or retain your individuality, your own identity throughout eternity. That's what this teaching has to offer, so you have to make that choice yourself. No one can make it for you. That which we think of as God is neither masculine nor feminine, but is referred to as IT, as a huge mass of atoms. It means one is unfolding in that neuter state, for neither man nor woman can go beyond the soul plane unless in the neuter state. This unfoldment cannot be seen, yet we can feel and sense it.

I am talking about the divine love, spirit, or of the Sugmad, and it is a great ecstasy in a sense, but it becomes subtler as one unfolds. As one goes through the various planes of existence, each plane has a different sound and a different color of light, until you get into the pure positive God worlds. There on the soul plane are different sounds, such as the subtle, haunting and melodious sounds of the flute and the bagpipes, and then the sound becomes much fainter and sometimes you wonder if you are still connected to the sound current.

Until you reach the God-conscious plane while here in the physical, you will find that not only does your life change for the better, but those loved ones around you that have resented your path or felt you were studying something of an occult nature, do not realize that this is the most ancient teaching and that all things spring from ITs source, all philosophies and all religions. This is something proven to each individual and does not have to be proven to anyone else.

How? By experience.

One factor that tends to hold man back is fear; it is one of man's evils. It can be overcome by filling yourself full of love. One of the marvelous steps on the path, is that the individual can overcome the fear of all things; he is not afraid of death, for death is one of those items that tend to hold us back in spiritual unfoldment. It stems from the way we have been taught, not academically, but spiritually and religiously.

Most families have been conditioned or taught to fear death and God. But who can really tell you or show you unless it has been experienced by that person and you can experience it yourself, not only to visit the lower worlds but also the pure positive God worlds?

Each individual who stays on that royal highway, not going too far to the right or too far to the left, will find that they will reach that goal, and can come back down and choose the plane which they wish to work from, and do far greater things than those man thinks of as miracles. But it is an individual path and your mate or family or your community may not realize what it is you are doing. That is why each individual must live his life in the way that suits him best and let others do the same, as long as they don't interfere with the psychic space of each other or others around them. The disruptive individual may feel he is living life his own way, but if his lifestyle disrupts those around him, he is interfering and will need to be removed or stopped from bothering others.

We must learn to live and let live by minding our own business. Even in our family situations. Other family members may not want to live as their parents do, or elders may not want to be shut away from the life stream. Let them do what they want to do. They can be reminded of their responsibilities to themselves and their family members, but if they choose to live a different lifestyle, let them go in good will. If there are consequences to pay, they will be the ones to pay them, no one else.

Man's fears include other people, his neighbors, his job, the beasts that roam the hillsides, or the insects that crawl on the ground, and even himself. Each survives on the same energy that unfolds the flower and that flows through each of us, and that sustains not only the Earth, but the galaxy and the universe, the structures of the heavens.

That's not saying you must embrace and love every person that crosses your path. We don't have to like everyone, yet we can love all life. We have to be on our guard with people and relationships, for those in lower states of consciousness may be more inclined toward the negative aspects of life. But you can be filled full of love for all life and still use common sense in your everyday dealings with individuals.

Each of us may develop this divine love differently. If

you have an attachment for an individual or a material thing, it is not divine love you are talking about, you have a physical love. It is with complete detachment that divine love unfolds within one, and this takes some doing. It may seem hard and cold to see a loved one going through something that you cannot help with, but by supporting him or her with divine love and letting it, Spirit, flow through you and surround you, it will reach that individual and be distributed, if not in your midst, then elsewhere, where it is needed most.

Sometimes when we are too attached to a person or an item of some kind, like a car or motor bike, it may be taken away from us, and very quickly and without warning. Sometimes it is not a very easy experience to go through that lesson.

When various groups pray for a Congressman, or the President, or for some bill they want to go through in Washington, D.C., they are interfering with that individual or factor, for no sooner will one thing be straightened out, than something else happens.

We do not know what is needed for the next person, or group of people. We cannot determine, know or want to set up conditions for another, because it will return to us as our burden.

If you want to write that Congressman, or the President, or you object to a particular bill being brought before Congress, do so in a letter or by personally appearing before these people to take a stand, but do not try to influence them psychically through prayers, for it is a violation of spiritual law, and will reverberate against you. The masses in general do not understand the power of prayer.

An example, and it is not for me to say it is wrong or right, yet when a person or group pray to rid a city of a negative situation, let's say, pornography (and I have seen this happen in many cities of the U.S.A.), the more that prayer is impressed upon an individual or a city, the more pornography is produced. I've seen this happen with so many issues of today in which men and women are praying the wrong way. Praying for that which they think is good for the whole nation, city, etc. Just stop and think about domination and prayer in Central America, and what has resulted from it. Do you want that for your nation?

Most do not understand the breaking of spiritual laws until they have had some experience with it. Once you have gained that awareness and gained that one factor of divine love, you carry it with you and it radiates, and people see and feel this.

The structure within the lower worlds, from the etheric worlds to the physical, is called action and reaction. The Lords of Karma (known as the Devil) control this and dish it out. Those who practice the spiritual exercises and the presence of the master or of God, unfold spiritually and move into that factor of divine love and are not affected by karma.

If they have a test to go through, they come out of it physically and spiritually stronger than we can imagine. Nothing holds you back except your own state of consciousness. Whenever individuals write that others are causing them grief, or that the spirit is not taking care of them, or another is creating situations they find hard to deal with, it shows that they are unaware that they themselves are creating these situations for

131

themselves. No one else can do anything to you unless you allow them to. If you allow an intruder into your space, even if it is a family member, you have only yourself to blame if that intruder upsets your life.

On Earth there are battles being fought today between nations, because of prejudice and greed. There are life forms, as we know life on other planets and in other universes, that some would think of as ugly or much different, yet they are very beautiful beings.

One city will differ from another city like London differs from San Francisco. Yet each difference becomes a difference in understanding of love.

When the children are ready to go out into the world, send them out with good will and love, with unattachment. Not indifference, with detachment, instead of admonishing them to be careful of this or that. Let them go and they will become greater human beings, and unfold spiritually as they experience life.

This is what it is all about. That is why we are all here-- for spiritual unfoldment, not for material achievements or other gains. Not for how much property we can gain or how much control we can have over others, but for spiritual unfoldment and experience. That is all we are here for; we are unable to make this planet as heaven is.

Even when people say, "Have a good day!" I answer back "I may not wish to, but with good will, I'll try." It's far greater. They don't know whether or not you want a good day. Someone may ruffle your feathers or upset you and you're not prepared for "Have a good day."

They don't really know and are just mouthing

meaningless words, but when you counter with: "With good will, I'll try," it gives them something to think about. And perhaps it helps them to see what they are doing and saying.

Another individual's ego becomes a "guest" in one's mental world and can create problems if allowed to stay there. This may be true for Christians who hold to Jesus as their spiritual leader. The entity becomes implanted within their being and grows within according to its nurturing.

Paul Twitchell details the "swarms" that develop within us as individuals in his writings, called "The Subjective Teachings." It is a fascinating aspect of our lives that few, if any, have ever known about before. As the modern-day messenger, Paul Twitchell gave us a yardstick by which to measure experiences, and brought into public view spiritual laws and factors that were purposely hidden away by those who chose to control the masses.

Paul Twitchell states: "We are individually the Supreme Consciousness of Itself, and need to recognize this fact. Soul is the central reality of the individual; Soul of Itself dwells in the ultimate cosmic consciousness, God-Realization, at all times."

Anyone who becomes a chela may not know at first what his true purpose is for entering into this path to God. But sooner or later, he reaches that state whereby experience will demonstrate that his sole mission is to reveal transcendental consciousness and thereby develop the individual consciousness to the place where he can truthfully say: "I live, yet not I, but the spirit liveth in me."

Unable to control his environment, the immature person's behavior pattern is much like the child who uses tantrums to gain what it wants. While we may not always be able to circumvent illnesses and obstacles that cross our paths, we can learn how to deal with them so they leave no devastating effects upon us. Each individual's experience in the spiritual realms will be individually different, according to what that individual needs to learn. So it is of no consequence for one to ask another about his experiences, for these will not help the asking person. Nothing from the "outside" will help another unless they use the yardsticks provided to seek and prove the answers through the inner experiences within themselves.

The most important key for the individual interested in his personal spiritual life and the universes around him is through the inner master. Until that acceptance is made, the individual can only go so far in his climb up the spiritual ladder. You do not have to believe what I say. But the average person does not know what he seeks or what his purpose in life is.

Those who hold discussion groups and classes should not fall into the trap of referring to the attendees as "my chelas." Whenever this happens, the class does not grow; their consciousness, collectively and individually, will not expand. That teacher is not functioning as a vehicle for spirit, but is trying to control the minds of the class. The master never refers to the chelas as his chelas, for they aren't. He is only the wayshower, the guide. He points the direction and then it is up to them to decide whether they are going to heed it. It is very subtle.

In soul, the choice is yours as an individual. You can retain your individuality throughout eternity and beyond. But if you choose to become one with God, that is your choice. No one is going to step in your way and say: "Hey, why don't you retain your individuality?" Only you and God know how you feel inside. There is no emphasis placed on the outer; you don't have to give up anything other than the little things inside that upset and disturb you. These are the things you ultimately give up, but it takes time to overcome some of what man calls "hangups," greed, anger, or what-have-you. There are no austerities practiced on this path.

Many will tell you how they have gained a freedom from situations of this world that arise on the street, at work or school, situations that are negative, that tend to pull them down in a state of consciousness. They rise above time, space and matter swiftly, more swiftly than the mind can grasp. They will not say much about their inner, personal experiences, but the initiate will tell you how their everyday lives have improved by learning to accept their responsibilities and cope with their lives.

In the long run, no matter how many lives it may take us to get to that point, we have to do it ourselves. No one can get you to "heaven" except yourself.

In all of the experiences of soul that are required for refinement, sometimes more than one lifetime is required. The following biblical references on reincarnation are given here:

Some come to me and ask to be taken to the God worlds immediately, and it is not up to me to judge whether that person is ready or not, for that is between the individual and spirit, which is the vehicle for God or Sugmad. That substance that supports all life is known also as Divine Love. Once you know how to release that soul body from the physical with your own volition, it moves swifter than the speed of light, many thousand times swifter, but what comes with it is something I cannot begin to tell you. These worlds are the pure positive God worlds.

Once man comes into the understanding or knowing, he doesn't have to fight for a piece of the ground. That same substance can be used to move his awareness.

There is no hurry or rush to gain the spiritual knowledge. It is so simple that once the intellect understands, you will find yourself saying: "Hey, I'll just be cool and listen, and one of these days I'll grasp it, some of the teachings."

The past teachers that have gone on are residing on

one of the lower levels of heaven and cannot assist the followers of their particular teaching. One needs a living master to take him through these worlds into the pure positive God worlds. You can read about this and doubt it, for I'm not trying to convince anyone. It isn't necessary. We don't try to pull anyone off their path or change their mind. We do not use mind control or any of the fear factors of guilt and sin to control anyone. It is breaking a spiritual law, and when we do that, even in ignorance, there are consequences to pay.

Somewhere, sometime; this is a law of God.

We don't beg for anything. There are various levels of consciousness and the person who has his hand out for money is at a very low form or position. Prayer is a step above that, and prayer, when practiced rightly can be used as a channel for God or spirit, which is God's vehicle to flow through us.

There are whole religious groups that pray for those in the cults, or me, and I feel it the moment it starts, as do many of the Initiates. They don't have permission to do this and it is sent back to them with divine love. There is no free, indiscriminate love on this path, no living in communes. Everyone must be responsible for their own thoughts and actions. We uphold the laws of man as well as the spiritual laws. There is no movement here to change this world or societies that exist within it. The truths of spirit are made available to all who are interested. The results are between the individual and the spirit of God.

The spiritual exercise that both Sri Paul Twitchell and I refer to most is The Easy Way, discussed in Brad Steiger's biography of Paul, In My Soul I Am Free, page

90, and detailed in my book, *Your Right To Choose*. It presents an opportunity for everyone to use a technique that, if practiced regularly on a daily basis, will move the individual out of his present state of consciousness into the inner realms of spirit. And trust in the fact that when this technique is being used, there is a spiritual traveler at your side as a guide and spiritual protector to keep you from being harmed.

At times the movement of soul can be startling and frightening, snapping one back to the physical body instantly, but this is not uncommon or unnatural. It is more natural for soul to run the physical body and mind than vice-versa, as has been the practice for most who seek for more than what they have now in life. One must be patient, both with the use of the technique itself, and with the results, even though "heaven is here and now." If you have a question about some aspect of yourself or your life, use this time of contemplation to become silent, chant or sing the word HU or some word of God that is comfortable to you, and look at the questionable aspect from every possible viewpoint. Look at it from every side possible. What you are doing is expanding your consciousness. Then don't hang on to the question; let go of it and it will be answered. However, remember when you are ready, the knowledge is yours.

Try not to become hung up mentally on material you read. When you read any of the books or any other works and have questions, move on. Suddenly something will open up and an answer will come when you least expect it. The material that is in written form is only to feed the mind for information, like a computer, to give one input, something to hang on to. You can learn how to drop all of the lesser bodies and move in the soul body if you wish to. But it must be used rightfully and for the good of the whole, for it will catch up with the individual who misuses the knowledge of spirit. This is the principle known as "as you sow, so shall you reap."

This is an individual and very personal relationship between you and God. No one is going to have any sort of control over you. Every step must be taken by you, yourself.

Meditation leads to the passive state, but contemplation can be done with the eyes open or closed, with the attention placed on the spiritual eye and not the belly button.

The initiate who does his homework and earns the right to notice and observe, through the initiations, the direction of spirit, is not going to misuse this substance, for it is greater than the atomic bomb by far.

We become a vehicle either for spirit or the negative power, and in order to have that divine love flowing through you, you have to get beyond the lower levels of heaven into the pure positive God worlds.

We do not have anything to do with the lower chakras or energy centers. We start with the crown chakra, at the temple within. It will take a lifetime for a person to work on a chakra at a time and then he is not assured of where he is going and will only wind up in the mental worlds at the most.

If the followers don't learn or know how to go beyond their body at the time of what man calls death (translation), they are still met by the master of the time and taken across, to the place where they have developed themselves spiritually. They continue to unfold from there, and they usually go very happy, and know that the master will be meeting them at the time of their passing. They do not have to go before the Lords of Karma, but are taken directly by the master to the level they have earned. Grief is not a pattern for the initiate, for translation or death is not a sad time for those on this path. It is a happy time because they are going on to greater experiences, and most understand this.

As some of you become more awakened, you will harness that energy for the good of all. The greatest thing that each and every person who chooses to be a vehicle for God can do, is to declare himself a vehicle for IT without directing that energy, and to let it flow through him, whether it is through a creative form or to assist the Mahanta. As you turn matters over to spirit, singing HU, things will smooth out. You are releasing that situation and becoming a vehicle for that which sustains life and letting it, via the vehicle, work through you. Sometimes it may look negative but don't misjudge. Go on to the next moment of time and on to the next phase of what you had set in motion, ignoring that past moment and whatever you had seen or heard.

You will find you can leave good will wherever you go without interfering with another person's state of consciousness and upsetting a particular cycle, and letting that person work through this cycle and become greater in your understanding of the divine spirit.

Our word as it is issued forth is recorded permanently.

Not only our thoughts, but what we say, and of course, our actions. Many have been aware of that strange feeling at some point of time in the pit of your stomach that something negative was taking place with a family member or someone close to you. It is the Inter Master warning you. I have direct knowingness with each and every chela on this path and with those that are taking a look at the teachings and what it has to offer the individual. If they decide to take that step, they are given the full spiritual protection and guidance and assistance, up to a point.

We can enjoy the relationships between our family and friends, but we must be careful of those thoughts we have about those around us. The airplane in the sky is using atoms, unmanifested souls, utilizing this energy which cannot be destroyed. As air goes through the jet engine, those minute particles known as unmanifested souls are pushed through, for an atom cannot be destroyed. These souls are at different levels of understanding and different levels of frequency and cannot be destroyed. One day we will be utilizing a vehicle that rides upon them but doesn't use them as the internal combustion engine does. We won't pollute the air.

Guy Murchie, in an article that appeared in Science & Music, wrote: "Music, particularly ultrasonic music in the presence of heat, has been found capable of changing the chemical structure and strength of crystals. But more fundamental is music's penetration to the very heart of the atom in the resonance principle, the revelation of which seems more and more to be establishing the concept that the smallest and most indivisible particles of matter may not realistically be considered nodes of resonance, which, in a sense, are poetically interpretable as living notes. Some physicists are even hopeful that the dynamic school of physical research (which mostly studies what happens when such sub-atomic particles collide) and the theoretical school (which mostly tries to categorize the same particles relative to their presumed least common denominator, the quark) will get together in a harmony they have never known, through acceptance of something called 'exotic resonance' (because it transcends quark harmonics) which now seems the most promising clue to the meaning of the complex symmetry of matter."

This resonance that is spoken of in Murchie's article is an aspect the masters have taught down through time and it is also written about by Paul Twitchell in The Flute Of God. The combination of the spiritual techniques of utilizing the practice of this resonance and the knowledge of enzymes is the key to longevity. Resonance nodes are unmanifested souls and when viewed through a prism they resonate at different frequencies, divided into colors, and can be used for modes of transportation.

The higher our level of understanding of the principles of the ancient teachings of the masters, the more ethical we become and the less we try to influence anyone, knowing each must experience life in his own way.

We learn to live and let live, minding our own business, yet giving divine love to all life.

Chapter 9

A SPIRITUAL GUIDE

To know one's self, as Socrates put it a few thousand years ago, is really the first commandment of the ancient masters. It is a great opportunity to make further discoveries in the universe and the heavenly worlds, for latent in man's brain is a capacity one million times greater than he is using now. Science has perceived that the average man of today uses only a small percentage of his brain cells.

This, the most ancient teaching in all of the universes, has been handed down through time by word of mouth until 1965 when Paul Twitchell began bringing its teaching out into the open through books and discourses. The master of the time, and those masters in the seven Golden Wisdom Temples have taught only those who were advanced spiritually to the point to be trusted in leaving the physical body temporarily while soul explored the worlds of this universe, including the planets and constellations or the invisible worlds where we go after the death of the physical body.

The teaching states that man has five bodies starting with the outermost sheath known as an aura or as the astral body. Surrounding the physical body is that starry and subtle body spoken of as the Nuri Sarup, the light body of the astral world. This is the outermost body demonstrated as an electromagnet sheath. It sparkles with millions of particles like stars shining in the universal heavens.

Within the astral body is another body, more subtle and much lighter, called the causal body, which is quite distinct from the astral. It is so named because it is the real cause containing the seeds of all that is ever to take place in the individual's life.

Another body is enclosed within the causal body called the mental body. It is more refined than the other two bodies. It would appear to the eye as a blue globe of light and has a humming sound when in the presence of another person. Its function is to act as a transformer for thought between the mind and the astral body. It is creative to an extent but only because it receives impressions from the etheric, or what is known as the subconscious part of the mind.

The etheric part of the aura lies between the mental body and the soul. It is regarded as the part of the mind body which acts as a sheath between mind and soul. It is very sensitive to impressions from soul and its function is to receive and transmit impressions between mind and soul on the one side and between soul and mind on the other.

A perfect record of every experience the individual has ever had in any incarnation within the countless ages of its existence throughout any plane is stored there. These can be read by the masters by use of what is known as the Vidya.

The fifth body which man has is many times spoken of as the atma sarup which is the soul body. It is an extremely sensitive body and in its natural state is a perfect vessel of the divine being.

144

Only by its compulsive lives in the bodies of the lower worlds does it appear to become imperfect. It becomes covered with a sheath making it seem imperfect but this is only the illusion of the negative forces that exist within the lower worlds.

These lower worlds I am speaking of start with the physical plane, and go on to what the scientists speak of as the Troposphere which is known as the astral world by the mystics and also within the God worlds.

The Tropopause on the scientific side relates to the causal plane in the teachings, and the mystics speak of the causal plane as the Brahmanda. The next plane is the mental plane known as the Stratosphere. The mystics speak of it as the Daswan Dwar. The etheric plane is known to the scientist as the Ionosphere. The soul plane to the scientist is the Unknown. The Vedanta speaks of it as a God plane, but it is the first plane coming from the Godhead or from the supreme deity known as Sugmad or God. The soul plane is the first plane of form as we know form, manifesting down into the lower worlds.

By the way, there is no negativeness whatsoever in the soul plane and beyond, but from the etheric plane down to the physical plane there are negative currents as well as the positive current. There are problems and power plays just as here on Earth.

The aura about the individual can be seen by those individuals who have developed the clairvoyant state or that which some speak of as expansion of consciousness to a certain point. The planes named above can be traveled to via the various bodies. However, having gone from the physical plane to the astral plane one must learn how to drop the astral body before going to the causal plane. From the causal plane, he must drop that body in order to go to the mental plane, whether he is traveling subjectively or objectively, in any of the worlds beyond the physical realm.

The initiates are taught to keep the physical, astral, causal and mental bodies intact, developing themselves only in the soul body.

Leaving the body via the Atma Sarup, often called out of body travel, is much different from astral projection which is well known in the annals of religion and occult sciences. This form of motion via soul differs mainly from the astral travel by the fact that we use the state of consciousness instead of any of the other subtle bodies, e.g., the astral, causal, mental bodies.

One might ask why it is necessary to travel to learn to use the soul body when he has an astral body that he could use, or a mental body.

Well, there have been many books written about these bodies, showing various astral bodies and mental bodies clouded, sometimes because of the emotional factor of anger or depression.

Man doesn't truly know that sometimes the things he might say or eat can also cloud what is known as the astral body or sheath.

For instance, tobacco and alcohol put dark spots in the astral body or literally open up a hole in it and let other negative currents flow through that body.

The individual that studies the works of this path learns how to close those holes up. It takes the individual self to do that. No other person can close up the hole, or you might say, adjust the aura of another person. There are those who have been charging a handsome fee for adjusting another person's aura and really haven't. They have lifted him in spirit or spiritually at the time, but that same hole exists, and shortly thereafter, the individual is right back where he started from.

In a book called The Tiger's Fang written by Paul Twitchell, he speaks of these bodies which man has, in relationship to the heavenly worlds, starting with the physical, astral, causal and mental as well as soul body, and he explains in this book the different levels that one can travel to, including other worlds that I personally have visited that one cannot find in any other writings or books within this world.

Most of those who are interested in the esoteric science are aware of astral traveling. The astral body is an exact duplicate of the physical body we wear except it is a much finer vibratory form and is connected with the imaginative faculty and emotions.

The consciousness is that state in which we have the ability to look, know and be.

When we travel beyond the soul plane, known as the fifth plane of God, into the higher realms of spirit, we will gain freedom, charity and wisdom. We can go anywhere we wish and do anything within reason under the authority of God. At least we are free of the lower world phenomena. The astral plane is, of course, a limited region. It is mainly concerned with the lower aspects of life, e.g., ESP, telepathy, levitation, astral traveling and psychic powers.

On the other hand, atma sarup travel, that is travel in

the soul body, leads to illumination, cosmic consciousness, and eventually to becoming a co-worker with God. It gives us the freedom to be anywhere we wish in the higher or lower planes, on any planet, or in this world of the Earth in this earthly form or invisible to others. It gives us a choice to help or not with people who are in need of spiritual assistance, but we do this under our own volition. In other words we can come and go at our own free will.

The students learn to leave their bodies much in the same way a dying man leaves his shell, except the neophyte does it voluntarily and the process is always under his control, and he can come back into the body at any moment he wishes to return. Otherwise his passing out of the body is practically the same as that of a dying man. He understands what death means and views what lies beyond death. He may even become acquainted with the astral home to which he is to go when he finally takes leave of his physical body.

He may also converse with friends and family who have long before left their physical bodies. This achievement cannot fail to interest the neophyte since it solves the gravest problems of life and destiny.

It is one phase of the great work of the Spiritual Travelers. They have broken the seal of death and so to them and their charges there is no more death. All of this is positive knowledge, not speculation or guesswork. Neither is it the interpretation of any book. It is through experience.

The individual who chooses to struggle along the spiritual ladder without the aid of a teacher or guide can only go so far without one. Once he reaches that point, it will be necessary to seek the Living Master to assist him through the tunnel of Yreka. The Living Master can also be seen on the outer as well as on the inner, which is rarely the case with other spiritual paths.

There is never a time in world history without a living master, although in the past, they kept their whereabouts secret, meeting on a one-to-one basis with the chelas, in order to survive.

The master can help the individual remove the heavy curtains of doubt, fear and illusion that have shrouded him for lifetimes. It requires the ability to surrender one's spiritual life to the inter master, the spiritual part of the master.

Usually by the time the individual meets with the master, either in the physical or in the dream state, it is because he or she has met all the requirements of a deep love, humility, and willingness to surrender to spirit. At that point, the chela begins the journey that will take him homeward, into the heart of God.

An interesting phenomena will sometimes occur with chelas who become aware of the Sound Current. Many have already heard the sound in various forms before ever hearing about these teachings, and in cases reported, they were very disturbed and didn't understand what they were hearing in their ears, for they had been blessed by spirit.

I have been approached by chelas who are disturbed by ringing in their ears or the occasional sound of crickets or bees humming in the distance. At their requests, I slowed down the sound current they were experiencing, not realizing the blessing they were actually hearing--The Voice of God.

Perhaps a month went by when a letter from one of these people asked me to please turn the Sound Current on again, which I did.

Another found that the sound current heard as the ringing of bells and roaring sounds of the sea were now under control and thanked me for the help.

While this divine gift is not readily accepted by some, to others, it is a "distraction" they are grateful to have in their lives. One called it "a life-line to spirit," and wondered how he could ever live without this precious sound within him.

This path is made up of everyday people who have been on one or more spiritual pathways throughout this life. There was, in some cases, divine discontent, for others, disillusionment and restlessness. Those who seek a curious new twist will probably not stay long on the path, for its very simplicity, its basic joyfulness, is too uncomplicated for them. Those in search of mental paths, logical mind patterns, will not succeed. The gift is given, however, one has only to accept the gift.

In Sri Paul Twitchell's book The Spiritual Notebook, he states:

"The point here is that truth, does not cause the chela's suffering; it is the false teachings that resist. Man loves to cling to something, and will happily hold closely to his breast anything that has been given him in the past through environment or teachings that might be alien to both his true nature and his spiritual progress, but he accepts them without question... when one keeps clinging to his old ideas the fight is only greater and prolonged."

Any individual who goes to that temple within and

150

asks questions, will find that, if his level of understanding can accept it, the knowledge is there. There is a vast amount of knowledge available to us, just for the taking, but we get caught up in the daily cycle of wanting to sleep five more minutes in the morning, or working or playing until bedtime, and allowing no time for the most important part of ourselves--the Inner Self.

The initiate learns to do a series of spiritual exercises that take from fifteen minutes to one-half hour a day. It entails quieting the outer self and placing the attention on the tisra til, the area between the eyebrows, and singing his secret word or the name of God--HU.

One can use any spiritual being he wishes as an image in the darkness of the mind screen, and should watch in an unhurried, relaxed manner for signs of the light and listen for the sound.

This can be very meaningful throughout the rest of that twenty-four hour cycle that will carry you through the day. In this manner you are creating a bond through the audible life current between yourself and the Inner Master, which ultimately will carry you to that experience that you desire. The experience of the light of the inner master usually comes first, and for some many times beyond that, depending on that individual's spiritual growth. It varies with each of us.

There is no one other than the master or yourself who can tell you where you are in your spiritual unfoldment. When I am told by chelas that they have no inner experiences, I know it is not true, for they are just unaware of what is transpiring within their inner worlds. The reality of it all is not coming through to the physical

151

body and mind. Such experiences are very subtle. When the inner master knows the individual will be at a certain place at a certain time for his spiritual exercise, the master will be there waiting for him, to assist him in whatever experiences the chela is requesting or towards that area that would be best for the chela's spiritual unfoldment and growth. The master is often kept waiting by others, but he never lets the chela down.

He lifts the chela by means of the sound current, often called the Bani, or Shabda, and the Word in the Christian Bible--that nectar of God that brings succor and that sustains all life, whether one realizes this or not. The bond made with the master is as great a bond as that which early man used to make with his neighbor--his word was his bond. No legal draftings were ever necessary, like they are now. If I commit myself to giving something that I have to another person, it is that person's property by my word. When I commit myself to meet someone at a given time, I am always early.

The development of this bond is what comes to you through the spiritual exercises and through unfolding yourself both in the spiritual worlds and the lower worlds, as well as in your physical life. As one becomes an initiate, and climbs the spiritual ladder, it becomes a very lonely journey. Don't let anyone kid you that it is all roses and fun. There are things you open yourself to that you cannot really discuss or talk to others about.

Those who go beyond the soul plane find it a lonely journey. To reach the experience of God-realization is the highest goal; however, it is uphill all the way by yourself with spiritual guidance as you request it.

The metaphysicians tell us we can have the material things in life just by asking God for them. I found that it didn't work like that at all as I was growing up. I found if I let go of what I wanted and where I wanted to be, it usually worked out, and maybe not always the way I thought it should be, but I always bettered myself and learned to think better of other people.

It is that radiant form, the light body, which is ageless and enduring, that which you really are, younger perhaps than you might be now, throughout eternity. Survival it is called. And remember the survival factors of joyfulness, happiness and having a cheerful heart from time to time, when you can. Keep a song in your heart is my motto!

When I first began having direct communication with Peddar Zaskq (Paul Twitchell), Rebazar Tarzs, and Fubbi Quantz, I would try to "out-do" them. And I couldn't, because they are swifter than the speed of light, swifter than the mind. Working from soul, it is very interesting--you know something before it happens.

I am referring to the time I was being taken to a Golden Wisdom Temple, reading the works from the wisdom temples, and thinking: "Gee, I can do this at work, and I can communicate with Fubbi Quantz," and of course, they let me know immediately that I had to use such knowledge rightly.

In order to take the next step, we are tested constantly. Sometimes we feel we are not being tested because nothing is happening, and perhaps we are not applying the proper initiative to make it happen. We may not have imagined the next step of our goal or our sights are not set high enough or we stopped off somewhere along the path. The choice is ours to make. But don't complain to the inner master or another individual about it. Don't judge yourself by what you see and hear others talking about.

This is one of the greatest mistakes man makes in this world--trying to judge himself by what he sees out there in the world, or hears with his outer ears, or what he hears others saying about their inner experiences.

If you want to travel with the Mahanta, as you drop off to sleep at night, call upon him and tell him you are ready and willing to take a trip tonight and imagine it. That experience of traveling with the Mahanta is just as great in the dream state, and sometimes it is difficult to tell what was a dream and what was waking reality.

Those who state they don't dream are stopping themselves, for everyone dreams, from the youngest to the most aged.

The masters work with the living master, not for selfish reasons, but for the good of all, no matter what planet people come from, regardless of their race or color of skin. It does not make any difference. They have given their lives over to the Supreme Deity to work as co-workers for the whole of mankind, on all planets and in all universes of Sugmad.

The gift is given to one and all alike.

Chapter 10

UNIVERSAL TEACHINGS

The teaching existed long before man existed on this planet. There has been groups or tribes living in the desert as well as other parts of this earth world. Most tribes found plenty of water, fruit, nuts, grain and meat. At times they took journeys out from their camps to find other people and other ways of life. They were adventuresome; some built boats to travel to distant shores. However, they went only far enough to return for they could get lost in the uncharted waters or in the desert. The travelers that came back had unbelievable stories to tell. At times they would return with grain, other foods that they had not known or had in their land. The travelers would tell stories of tall grass, green fields, rain and mountains. The people thought these travelers told great fairy tales. They did not believe them.

One young man who was adventuresome wanted to find out if this traveler was speaking the truth and went with him on one of his journeys. Lo and behold, he found what this man had talked about earlier. The land of green fields, plenty of sunshine, mountains and rain did exist. He could not wait to get back to his band of people and tell them. But they did not believe him.

It is often this way. A spiritual traveler will meet you, or spirit will touch you, or an individual, and you can be walking down the street seeing someone jump for joy and this is caused by contact with a master's presence. Once an individual travels to this state of God-consciousness and comes back down to the soul plane while residing here on this physical realm of being, he has had an experience that is very difficult to talk about. Who will believe you? You want to shout it to the world but you cannot.

The individual who seeks to ride that cosmic sea, to go beyond the physical realm of being, to get above the lower worlds, can do this by going to that temple within. But do not stop there; it is the starting point.

A lot of the teachings that man has had on this planet through the past centuries have either led him into wars or into a passive state to where he sat still and did nothing. Yet the initiate, those who follow this path, can and do learn how to sit still and do something.

Very few understand or learn how to achieve this state, yet it has been handed down from the masters to the chelas ever since man has been on this planet as well as on other planets. And this teaching derives from the one Supreme Being and the soul plane, coming from the pure positive God worlds down into the lower worlds.

I have become more accustomed to various flows of energy and studied them for fourteen years in the science field. I thought I had a pretty good handle on it.

Designing transformers and magnetic components used to be my specialty. Many times I was accused of eating pickles and ice cream before going to bed at night because I'd wake up in the morning with some weird ideas that worked.

Reaching into the astral plane is fairly easy, for that is

where all of man's inventions derive from.

The greater creative activity on this planet, such as painting, music, and other arts and art forms, originates not only from the astral plane but from the causal, the mental and etheric planes, and in the higher worlds a still greater flow of energy exists.

When a chela or an individual out on the street, or in a restaurant, becomes excited and happy for a moment, the spirit has touched that person, for you can count on a master having walked by.

There could have been a master walking down the street, or the individual might have been in the presence of a carrier of spirit, you might say, in the presence of a chela sitting next to that person or in that room, and this flow of energy which has flowed through a channel touching the individual who is ready or has been seeking.

We cannot, as ourselves in the human body, say we want that which is spirit and force it, because it has selected each and every chela who is on this path.

It works in various ways which the initiates themselves learn to understand wholeheartedly; not by pushing, not by forcing, but by being themselves as individual human beings, expanding their consciousness without the use of anything other than their own faculty, taking that contemplative thirty minutes a day.

This is what western man has a difficult time doing-- being able to sit still. I know--I had the same problem.

This is a spiritual freedom, a freedom that in the human state of consciousness one cannot understand totally. You can read about it and still not totally understand it. Nor can it be described in all of man's words. The early mystics and holy men tried to describe it, tried to tell their followers about it. They were unable even in body gestures and movement to do so, but some of their dances derived from this great current which sustains all life. It takes discipline, which no one else but the individual himself can place upon himself.

Self- discipline in all things, maintaining the balance so that one doesn't go too far to the right or to the left is necessary, and sometimes it is not easy. It is spoken of in man's scriptures as the narrow way. It is really the razor's edge. When the narrow edge on the path has been reached and one has gone beyond that point, one finds the path becomes lighter for him.

This is getting through the tunnel of Yreka on the etheric plane and going into the soul plane, where all individuals, regardless of what path they are from, must accept the master as a spiritual guide if they have developed themselves to that point where they are ready to have their spiritual legs planted on the soul plane. Then they shall be taken through by the master.

The Mahanta, the inter master, is the vehicle. But the tunnel of Yreka is where some people stop.

Many paths of self-realization or those that know how to get to the soul plane think that it is the ultimate heaven. Some of the paths and teachings have their lord or their God established on the first astral plane.

This is very difficult for some to accept or believe, and I do not ask anyone who disagrees with that to accept my statement. You can read about it, but you still do not have to accept it. However, if you are truly interested in developing yourself spiritually, you can experience it. You can know for yourself which no one else can do for you.

It takes a struggle to start back up some of the paths that you have climbed reaching this point, and to reach for a higher level yet. It isn't easy, but the rewards are great, greater than one can really comprehend in the negative state known as mind. One must drop all of the bodies and step out into the life force itself; as the Bible states, one must separate soul from the physical body.

A great number of individuals know of some of the lower bodies but do not know how to keep them intact, as the masters of the teachings. They teach the chelas to keep the physical body along with the astral, causal, mental and etheric body as one body, and use the soul body only, be it on the other side of this continent, or working off the soul plane and going for the God-conscious state or to heal someone, someplace.

Many have asked me to help them go out beyond themselves, but very rarely will I do this. I will meet the chela and am always at that door (the Tisra Til), not in my physical body, but in the soul body. You can see me in the dream state or on one of the higher planes as an inner master.

If you are happy on the path you have now, do not try and mix this teaching with any other teaching. It will cause great difficulties. One creates great frustrations mixing two paths. If you are bold and adventuresome and not satisfied with the path you have been a part of, investigate, but don't mix two paths at one time.

Those who take the initiation become attuned to a greater amount of the audible life stream, and find they can really start to develop themselves spiritually.

Usually a greater amount of the sound current is given to the chela with the initiation, but many times the master has given it beforehand, knowing the chela is going to be performing as a co-worker on the path.

The physical plane is the universe in which we live, the area of illusion of reality, of Maya, of day and night. This is the lowest vibration to which you as an individual have developed at this point, and where you now reside.

Above the physical plane is the astral plane. There are some lower astral planes between the physical and the pure astral worlds. It is in these regions that man, through his religions, has established his "hell." It is a dark area where one who commits murder or some crime must work off his karma when he leaves this physical plane of being, before getting into the high astral plane.

The pure astral plane is at a higher rate of vibration than this physical one. The colors are greater, yet the structures are very similar to those seen in the physical world, only at a higher rate of vibration.

This is the source of all psychic phenomena, spirits, astral projections, flying saucers, etc. The ruler on this plane is Kal Niranjan. The scriptures on this planet speak of him as Satan or the devil. He is not to be feared, however, just understood.

The Chinese or Eastern teachings speak of the lower world as the Yin and Yang, the positive and the negative. This negative current or power is just as important as the positive in these lower worlds. It is used for creativity, whether it is the building you reside in, this planet or your physical body. We should understand this negative current and learn how to balance with it, just as with the positive. No one can raise the individual above these two currents into the pure positive God worlds except the masters.

When I first experienced the astral plane, I thought I was in heaven and didn't want to come back to the physical. I knew my way around quite well. I learned about the lord or ruler there, about the Golden Wisdom Temple there, where I received some schooling, and about the knowledge that exists there which man is seeking and which is unavailable in any of his books on this planet.

Yet all of Man's basic scriptures and philosophies have derived from the set of books on each and every plane of God, clear through to the soul plane, The Way of The Eternal.

The causal plane is the area in which Kal Niranjan himself resides and from which he rules these lower worlds. He is at the negative or bottom pole and his function is to hold soul within these lower worlds.

The causal plane is the seed body of all the past and future experiences you and I have had and will have throughout our many lives.

The mental plane is known by the mystics and by those who are able to travel these lower worlds. It is the realm of Brahm or Brahmanda or Jehovah. This is the source of all man's philosophy, ethics, moral teachings, conventional "God" and religion.

There are about eighty different continents here and each one is as marvelous as the next. Kipling wrote about it. He was adept at reaching into this area while existing in the physical body and described some of these continents in his writings.

Paul Twitchell is the first who has brought information about this plane out in the detail that he has. Most of the mystics, saviors and saints tried to tell Man about it but very few really believed them. This stemmed from the way Man has been taught down through the centuries. He has been held back.

The social structure in which we live, the rules which Man has made, which we must abide by while we reside here, has been set up to control the masses. This should not be a surprise to most people. I do not have to prove this to anyone because one can prove it to himself, through experience, and when you know, you know! The individual that chooses to be freer than the human mind can begin to comprehend. That sincere student who develops himself spiritually will know.

The etheric plane is the unconscious part of Man. It is a very thin world between the mental world and the soul plane. It is the source of the primitive, and is the greater part of the mental area of Man. Through hypnosis he is trying to learn more about himself and about his past lives.

However, there is a more efficient way, and that is dropping the etheric body completely, getting beyond it and working from the level of the soul plane.

On our sojourn through these lower worlds, which is known as the Wheel of Eighty Four and that which the zodiac is set up on, we continue along that wheel until we either have developed ourselves spiritually as an individual, or have met a Spiritual Traveler who is on the path of the ancient ones.

If an individual has learned through hard knocks and through study that there is life beyond this physical realm of existence, and chooses and cries out in desperation for certain experiences, and has been floundering, a master usually will watch over that individual and guide him onto the path.

If you should be working off the astral or causal or mental planes, and you get off on a tangent and are happy there, I'm going to leave you and let you be happy. Because if you can have a moment of happiness, grab it; latch onto it.

When you are ready to swing back to that middle path where you are not going too far to the right or the left once more, I'll put you back on it when asked.

The teachings take you above these lower worlds, above time, space and matter, to where all is omnipresent, omnipotent, and omniscient.

The moment you step onto the path, via the study program, the Masters within the Golden Wisdom Temples move you in your soul body, as fast as you are capable, to the soul plane.

Many times this happens and the individual doesn't realize what is taking place and fear sets in. This fear stems from lack of understanding, understanding yourself as an individual, a lack of intellectual understanding. Then there is Self-Realization, a complete understanding of yourself as a human being, and lastly, God-Realization.

Within the orthodox teachings or the various teachings like the occult, there are terms such as Christ-Consciousness, or Cosmic Consciousness,

163

These are not Total Awareness. They are steps, however; if you have reached them, don't stop there because there are planes beyond what you see. Once one reaches the Hukikat plane, this is the highest one as an individual soul can go while still occupying a physical body. This is the God-conscious state.

The choice is yours alone as to whether you will work on the soul plane in your soul body while residing here, or on one of the lower planes. The soul body has no age, is indestructible and can transcend time, space and causation. We have been taught how to grow old and how to die, but not how to stay young and how to live. But you will find and learn, as well as read, that God of ITself does not care for the physical body, which is just a few pints of blood and a clay shell.

In traveling from the physical realm to the astral plane, you can drop the astral body and go on to the causal in a second. The Living Master and the masters who reside here on this physical plane of existence, such as Rebazar Tarzs, Fubbi Quantz, and Yaubl Sacabi, bypass all of these lower worlds and are able to go directly to any plane they wish to, swifter than the mind can grasp.

While these Masters live and serve the lower realms of existence for mankind, they work with aspiring individuals through the soul body, although they have been known to appear at various seminars as viewers. They disappear if they are approached, for their work with chelas remains on the inner realms.

Man believes light is the fastest form of speed, but it is not. Light travels on the current that sustains all life. This current from the Sugmad, or from God, as known by the conventional teachings, is stepped down at each level, objectively as well as subjectively. There is a ruler on each plane. That ruler is subject to the Supreme Deity or the Sugmad. Even Kal Niranjan is subject to the laws of God. The various rulers on these planes in the lower worlds are subject to karma and reincarnation, just as the entities that reside on the various lower planes.

Until I was fortunate to meet with Gopal Das and read the Shariyat-Ki-Sugmad on the astral plane, I doubted that the basic scriptures of man derived from that set of books. After reading several of these books, the doubts faded away, because the knowledge that is contained within that set of books does not exist anywhere else. They have existed longer in time than man knows of.

A set is kept in the Katsupari Monastery in northern Tibet, which is on the physical plane. The next set of books is on the planet Venus. One goes in the soul body to visit Rami Nuri, the Master in charge of that Wisdom Temple.

In the spiritual city of Agam Des, Yaubl Sacabi is in charge of the next set. He has many functions; he watches over this whole universe. Any flying saucers from the astral plane or perhaps another planet must pass through this spiritual city and the passengers must lower their vibrations if they are taking on a physical body to walk on this Earth plane.

There is a vast amount of knowlege available for the masses, but Man does not understand himself, let alone the world or universe in which he lives. Very few partake of this knowledge, nor the ration or amount allotted to them. I wondered about that when I first heard of it as I was going to the Gobi Desert over in northern Tibet for some schooling with the Master, Banjani.

Then when the individual has reached a point where he has both feet firmly planted on the soul plane and is adept, and has made God-consciousness his goal, he is turned loose. There is no holding him back. Some find themselves very much alone, suddenly without friends and seemingly without any power. Yet they have a power flowing through them that most would like to know about.

Later when I became more adept at out of body travel and read my own soul records, I found that some of the high points of the past lives were such that I wouldn't want to talk about them today. This is why Rebazar Tarzs states to Paul: "Don't look to the past nor to the future. Live this moment the best you can." It cannot be simpler.

All of the great scriptures are marvelous for starting to open up the consciousness, as well as any of the passages. However, this is only a starting point. There is no greater temple to start from than that temple within. All of the teachers on this Earth plane have stressed this from before Socrates and since. Many have become aware of Rebazar Tarzs or Fubbi Quantz, after Peddar Zaskq (the spiritual name for Paul Twitchell) brought knowledge of them to the world through his writings.

When Columbus hit the shores of this country, he was guided by the Master Rebazar Tarzs. The western man, especially in this country, thinks that he has the greatest material thing going for him, yet the eastern man has him beat. He has the jump on the western man because he has been at it a little longer and is perhaps a little more spiritually developed as some think, yet none can tell you, or any race, where they have unfolded to spiritually.

Once you meet one of the masters who reside within one of the Wisdom Temples or the other planes, or the Living master, your whole life changes and you will find that if you are able to let go and turn the problems and troubles over to the inner master on the inner planes, your life straightens out and you begin making gains for the first time. You know without question that you are on the right highway, that it leads uphill.

There are tests, and the higher you go the more frequent they become. Many individuals find after stepping onto a spiritual path, occult or religious, that they will have some negative experiences, and this can happen on the path. However, don't let that stop you. You will find that the masters are the only ones within the physical realm of existence that can raise you above good and evil.

There are masters and teachers on other paths, but they must all come to one of the masters when they reach the tunnel of the Yreka, which is the area between the unconscious (or etheric) and the soul plane. This was set up, not by the masters but by Sugmad itself. That is why you will find initiates do not put down any other spiritual path. If you are on a spiritual path and happy there, stay with it. If you have not learned all you want to know, however, and are interested in learning where you are going, how to get there, and what you are going to do, you shall learn.

You will find in the original word, HU, is the father of all motions, forces, lights, sounds and elements that subsequently come into existence in the fifth plane and belong to IT. It is the secret name for God; the spirit current, the prime mover and the first impulse that came from the Deity and also the first cause of motion, color and form.

Authoress Arianna Stassinopoulos, interviewed in The Philadelphia Inquirer, April 7, 1981, about her bestseller biography on Maria Callas, told of her morning meditation, "using an ancient Sanskrit word, HU," which, she said, is the oldest word for God. She wears a necklace with HU spelled out in delicate gold filigree.

The article continued by saying: "She has been meditating for the last six years. It helps to keep everything in perspective...It's really like focussing on that part of ourselves which is forever, which exists independently of the ups and downs, the successes and the failures."

Paul Twitchell expressed this about HU in his writings. It is this kind of faith or inner awareness and openmindedness, which finds its spontaneous expression, its liberation from an overwhelming psychic pressure in the sacred sound of the HU. In this mantric sound, all the positive and forward-pressing forces of the human, which are trying to blow up its limitations and burst the fetters of ignorance, are united and concentrated on spirit, like an arrow point.

It is the first and most important task to bend and restring the bow of soul by proper training and discipline. After the self-confidence of discipline has been restored, the new doctrine has been firmly established, and the ornaments and cobwebs of theology and metaphysical speculation have withered and fallen before the sacred word of HU, It can again be attached to the spiritual exercises.

Paul, in telling about the Earth's beginnings, relates that the Satya Yuga was a time of peace and happiness for Man, that the land of Lemuria contained highly civilized and enlightened peoples until black magic brought about the destruction of this great empire. The mantra of the HU was the sacred chant of all the people in the Satya Yuga.

It was a manifold of conscious patterns contrived to assist the consciousness into the patterned world perceived. Because spirit was the greatest force of these times, it was maintained for 1,728,000 years before the Tretya Yuga or the silver age took over.

There are techniques and principles to live by. Most of the time in the physical and human state of consciousness, the relationship between the different spiritual worlds and the physical worlds is not totally understood by mankind.

The principles of spirit have been included in many of my writings. There is no other path that can give the succor from the Sugmad that flows from the pure positive God worlds down through and including this physical plane, except through the Mahanta, the Living Master. The Mahanta and I are one, yet I do not direct IT. I let that flow through, for I have been taught how to go and come directly, which all chelas that are serious are able to do in time.

Maybe only one in a hundred will make it, but the possibility is there. The inner light is knowledge, is the Mahanta, the inter master. It has always been and always will be visible as the blue light or blue star.

You will find that I am as close as your breath and as near as your heartbeat. But according to spiritual law, the Master will not enter into your life unless he is invited, even though you are never alone. There is always some spiritual being watching over you, ready to assist you in time of stress and trouble.

The Creed states: "All life flows from the Sugmad, downward into the worlds below, and through them, and nothing can exist without this cosmic current known as Divine Spirit, which can be heard as sound and seen as light.

The basic principles are:

1. Divine Spirit is the ancient, original essence which sustains life in all universes.

2. The ancient teaching that is the source from which all religions and philosophies spring.

3. The Living Master is the only manifestation of the Sugmad on Earth, and the basis of his teachings lie in the Inner Master.

4. The Living Master's only mission is to gather up Souls who are ready, and start them on the path to God again.

5. The Living Master is the perfect instrument of the Sugmad on this plane; often he is the Mahanta. His duty is to make every soul who comes to him realize he has only one mission in life, and that is to return to God and likewise become an instrument of God."

(Taken from The Spiritual Notebook by Paul Twitchell.)

Chapter 11

THE ART OF SURVIVING

As a child I was taken to my mother's church where someone stood behind that podium and pounded on it, trying to scare everyone in the pews. We do not use those tactics; we want you to understand yourself and how to overcome all fear, the fear of all things. Most of all to gain that knowledge that is needed for survival throughout eternitiy--of where you are going, of what you are going to do, and most of all, how to get there.

This is having control of one's own destiny, not letting others control us as individuals. It is a real spiritual freedom for the individual. Not for a nation or country, but for the individual who is ready for the next step, and who works for it and earns it.

I remember being told as a youngster that if I asked for certain things and prayed for them, they would be given. I'd pray very hard for two or three months for something and it never happened, and I didn't realize that the things I was looking for and wanted to happen in my life had to be earned. The same law that exists here on this physical plane exists in what man calls "heaven." And those things we desire and want in our life spiritually must be earned and worked for in some manner. This isn't totally understood by most of the leaders of the masses or the religious orders.

Metaphysicians tell us we can have material things as

well as spiritual things, but they don't tell us that we must pay for them in return. This is why some individuals go along for a period of time, whether meditating or praying, or living their life the best they know how, and all of sudden the whole bottom drops out. All the positive powers of thought, even if one is practicing the mind dynamics, head in a downward curve because we are not taught how to move in our soul body in states of consciousness, in order to rise above these situations that come up.

Whether moment by moment, day by day, on the street or at work or in the home, at school or on the play yard, this shifting of states of consciousness happens, and we have little youngsters in grade school, and some not even in school yet, who are great little spiritual travelers. They move about on the other side while they are here, gaining further spiritual knowledge, as do some of the adults.

Most everyone has read or heard about the mystics, saints and saviors who have stressed the separation of soul from the physical body. St. Paul, the Apostle, spoke of this as "I die daily," and in II Corinthians, stated: "I knew a man in Christ about fourteen years ago (whether in the body I cannot tell; or whether out of the body I cannot tell: God knoweth); such a one caught up to the third heaven. How that he was caught up into paradise, and heard unspeakable words, which it is not lawful for a man to utter."

St. Paul was a member of the Order of the Masters, and when he was ordered executed by Nero, he stretched out his neck on the swordsman's block and said: "I must die, but no, it is not I that dies. It is only the body that takes the sword blow and dies. I am imprisoned within this pit of clay and the sword shall release me from it forever. I shall live hereafter in the true glories of God."

Plato, another Master who worked in secret with the chelas, spoke of separation of soul from the body, and wrote of the "purification" technique Socrates used in Plato's *Phaedo*, which was actually the separation of soul from the body without going through exercises, concentration or meditation.

More about the masters of the ancient order, many of them famous men of history, can be found in The Spiritual Notebook by Paul Twitchell. Some of the encounters I have had personally with the masters are in my biography. They are very real people, just as alive as you and I are. They dwell in the physical and higher realms of God, depending upon the area they have chosen to work in. Many of them work directly with the Living Master of the times, assisting with the teaching and training of the chelas under his care.

The separation of soul from the body used to be well-known and used by the ancients. This knowledge has been lost as to how to do it and with ease, without drastically affecting our way of life.Out of body travel deals with the movement of body, moving within this physical universe or into the astral, causal, mental, or the etheric plane, as far as one can travel with the lesser bodies, the ones other than the soul body.

The subtlety of the soul, once the individual steps out of this clay shell, is developed by the individual as he works with the master, who guides him through the inner worlds. Once all the lower bodies are dropped and the chela has found his way to the soul plane and develops himself in the soul body, he has learned all he can from that position and is turned loose by the master. It is then up to the individual to go on to the God-conscious state from there, for no master worth his salt will hold on to any chela. There are several more layers or levels of existence, beyond the soul plane, as discussed earlier, one being the invisible world, then the endless worlds and then into the God-conscious plane. That is as high as one can reach in his soul body while here on this physical plane of existence, insofar as developing one's self spiritually.

This travel is within this physical realm and on up to and including the etheric plane for those who learn how to do this. But once you reach the soul plane, there is no movement as we know it. It is the first plane of form as we know of "form," coming from that which is known as God or IT.

IT is greater than one can imagine, in the form of light and the atom structure. The energy from that plane is stepped down to each of the levels and there is a ruler on each of these levels.

As Paul Twitchell wrote in The Tiger's Fang, his report of his own personal journey through ten different levels of heaven, the descriptions of these journeys are guideposts to show the individual what particular plane he may be working off while still residing in the physical body. Such as the color of the plane one might see subjectively within himself as he is unfolding or objectively as he is traveling. There is a sound on each of the planes. When one starts to go beyond himself and partakes of what is known as the Shabda or

174

Sound Current, that which sustains all life, he may hear thunder or a cannon going off somewhere behind him during contemplation.

That is why no one else can tell you where you are spiritually. We are here only for unfoldment and experience, and who can tell you your unfoldment or experience but yourself and the master who acts as spiritual guide, instructor and teacher?

The masters are spoken of as the Godmen, the messengers of God, yet like myself, they are human beings on the physical plane, getting colds, aches and pains and needing nourishment in their physical bodies.

The only thing we can take with us when we drop this physical body is the knowledge we gained while we were here, and those who develop this aspect we all have within ourselves. The only thing you will receive is the ability to know, and when you know, you know. No one can take that from you. That is your survival factor. You've heard people say: "I don't know why I know, but I DO!"

There is often a deep longing that exists within mankind, a fire that remains kindled until it is extinguished through proper spiritual guidance. There is no sweeter wine or nectar that man knows of, yet it is not for the masses. It is for that individual who is bold and adventuresome, who does not take everything for granted that he hears or reads. For the one who has doubts and who can question.

I have told the story of the lady who dropped out of the church because she was still seeking something she was not getting in church. The meditation group she joined next could only take her so far, so she began to work on her own. All of a sudden during her quiet hour, this light appeared within her and out of it came a voice that said: "I am the Great One!" Startled, she asked: "The Great One who?" The voice replied: "The One you have been seeking!"

She listened and found she could learn much from this light and one day her teacher revealed to her that he was Shamus-i-Tabriz, the master who works off the causal plane. She had learned to develop herself in the form of travel from the physical to the astral, dropping the astral body, and going to the causal plane, where many individuals are able to read their Akashic Records while working off the causal plane. But she wasn't happy with that, just being able to look back at the past and read the past records of Earth or herself or anyone else who had asked her to. So she continued her growth in her search with this master at her side.

The temple within is a starting place only. We should not linger there. We are the microcosm within the macrocosm, with suns, moons, duplicate replicas of that which exists in the outer worlds. We can work off certain karmatic patterns and conditions that have come about through other lives, and that plague us here. If one has a situation that needs resolving, it can be handled in the dream state, keeping it from coming into the physical realm. Or it can be worked out while one is at work, the result being that what has been set up to happen won't come about. Something else will take place for the better, for the good of all concerned, once this is learned.

The individual can help himself in his material life, and beyond the capability of imagining with the mind in spiritual unfoldment. There is nothing held back even though the teaching is secret. I'll explain that secret part. The only thing that will hold one back is his own state of consciousness, because this is the only thing worth consideration--the expansion of our consciousness without drugs or objects or anything other than yourself.

Some come onto the path and unfold swiftly while others take several years to attain this ability. There are at least 25 or more techniques in the books and discourses and any one of them can help one expand his state of consciousness. Remember, though, this deals with placing the attention on something desired or the place to be visited, visualizing the goal desired, and then relaxing and letting go. Some try these spiritual exercises a couple of time and give up because they feel nothing happens. Since the spiritual aspects are subtle, it requires patience and trust and sincerity before one may be aware of having had any experiences. But whether they are aware of this physically or mentally or not, it is still happening.

In order for one to become a greater and more useful vehicle for the spirit to use, one must be cleared or one's bodies purified of certain aberrations carried over into this lifetime by karmatic debts from previous lives.

A good share of this is worked off in the first two years of study on this path, and the individual then chooses whether or not he wishes to return to the physical plane to assist as co-worker in his next life.

As one can see, the choice of each and every step

all along the way is up to the individual himself. No one is ever forced or pushed into anything. It would be a violation of spiritual law to do so. Many religious orders force their wills upon their congregations, by using fear tactics and guilt as control factors.

When we try to feed a young child something he doesn't want, he balks and you usually get his food all over yourself. Think of the consciousness as the neck of a small bottle. You can only put so much liquid into that bottle at one time, and until the neck of the bottle is either widened, or the bottle emptied, it can only hold so much. Once the vehicle can hold more, a great amount of knowledge is made available for its use

There are things we learn from childhood to adulthood that tend to hold us back spiritually. Now, how does one learn about this? It is on an individual basis. It isn't up to anyone to judge another, for we cannot tell through our physical eyes where another is spiritually.

It is very seldom that the master of the time will take upon his shoulders the burdens or karmatic debts of his followers. Occasionally, if there is a function for that person somewhere in the physical universe or this world, he might take a portion of that person's burden and turn it over to spirit to be worked off very swiftly, and the individual involved rarely knows this. It is up to us as individuals to have certain experiences. We cannot place excessive attention on the outer worlds and expect to have greater spiritual knowledge.

Working with the spiritual exercises, you can bypass the lower worlds. However, you can spend time looking at the earth records or visiting the Wisdom

Temples on the lower planes. You can see where the flying saucers are coming from, and where various paths have their deities, but you don't tear apart another's faith in his path, or put it down.

We are not here to hassle anyone or throw rocks at anyone. This teaching is for the individual who wants to go directly to that known as God while he is here alive in this plane of existence, to experience these other worlds and dimensions and become adept at finding the answers that man has been seeking for centuries.

There have been a few who have had this knowledge, but they kept it from the eyes of the masses. If opened up to all, it would be like turning a bank over to a little youngster. He wouldn't know what to do with it. He'd go out and buy all the lollipops and sodas and that sort of thing, and what good would it do? This is true with this vast amount of knowledge and energy that is available--man would destroy himself.

This current spoken of as Shabda, or that we know of as Spirit, that sustains all life, is a catalyst and the binding force of the universe. Through the initiations, the individual, if he is ready for it, is given more of that which already sustains him. It is up to him how he further develops himself and makes use of this creative current which is active, not passive.

Some individuals become a vehicle for it and aren't aware of it. It is important to become a clear vehicle, not trying to direct it in any manner or impress it upon another person or nation, but let it work through one for the good of all. Once one starts to do that, he finds he is doing miracles that he cannot even talk about to his loved ones. He cannot mention it to anyone else he comes in contact with. He may be working in various areas and doing things that others just read about.

I'm not saying that the written word will have all the answers for all of us. For some, yes, but that person who doubts, like I did, may become a greater believer because he is shown through his own efforts.

There is no language with which one can attempt to talk about the pure positive God worlds, no music, no picture that can be painted to describe them, but they can be experienced. Sometimes it is through the youngsters that we are shown where we, as adults, have fallen short. They also point out to their elders the conditions of our waters, the pollution in the air. Many of the younger people are from the early Roman and Grecian era and are rebelling a bit, and we have to bend a little with them. This is taking the middle path.

Not going too far to the right or left. Then one day you find you have come to that rung on the ladder known as the Dark Night of Soul. You will think all heaven and earth and everyone in it has left you, including the Master or the spiritual guide you have.

From that point it is touch and go. St. John spoke of his Dark Night of Soul, and anyone can get a glimpse of what sort of difficulty one can go through.

Others do not experience this deep negativeness and hardship. It is not necessary. Atoms who learn to die daily, overcome the fear of death quite swiftly. This is a factor in survival. Some of the eastern teachings impress upon man to become one with God through meditation. But initiates will experience God and retain their individuality throughout eternity, and choose themselves what type of work they want to do in the worlds of God. Whether they want to come down into the lower worlds to become a cherub, or work with the Lords of Karma, there are thousands of opportunities, and this choice, again, is the individual's.

It involves learning not only about yourself, Self-Realization, but going to the next step spoken of as cosmic-consciousness or Christ-consciousness by many teachings. The ultimate step and everyone's goal eventually will be God-consciousness while here in this physical realm, experiencing it themselves.

There has always been one known as the Vi-Guru. Regardless of what path an individual comes from, if he has developed himself to that point and is ready, he goes through and is taken through the tunnel of Yreka. Some choose to spend time in the mental world, spoken of in Kipling's works as fantastic and beautiful.

It has 80,000 continents, and one can choose to travel to and stop at each one of those points. No one will pull him back to the middle path, but one day he, himself will become restless and discontented and want to continue on.

It is in the mental worlds where one reaches that fork in the road, where one can go straight ahead, or to the right or left, and where he has the choice of using black or white magic. He learns that black magic leads to destruction. That is the only way one can lead himself to destruction.

If he chooses the middle path, he will find the bliss and joy of the soul plane that has been written about for centuries. But it is not the Ultimate Being who resides there. The Being there is known as Sat Nam, the ruler of the soul plane.

The records of one's self are stored in the causal or seed body; these are lesser records, the records of the past. But around the heart area and in the soul body, you will find that the records of each life that you have lived are like little cards that can be fanned out like a playing deck. From start to finish, each event is recorded on a card for each of your lives. When I reached the soul plane, I found it was fairly easy to read my own records. I did not read them all. why? Too many of them.

I don't read anyone's life or soul records because it is quite a task to separate the various magnetic fields, and one must know what one is doing if it is to be done properly. It takes about eight million, four-hundred thousand lives to make one complete cycle on that zodiac wheel, and most of us have been around at least once. I don't ask anyone to believe me because that person who doubts and questions, looks at and tests all this, will find out for himself or herself.

I had to do the same thing, because I was taught as a youngster not to believe everything I read or heard. If we can teach our children today not to be for or against anything, they will grow up to be greater creative individuals, yet they will have their opinion about situations and things. They won't go around misjudging or prejudging. It is very essential that we look at things from a 360-degree viewpoint, rather than a narrow 10% or a 20% angle. Once one starts to break out, it is like a pair of eyes at a point over here looking back at yourself. Then in your spiritual growth and development you reach to the area where you move swifter than your mind can grasp--and you KNOW.

You know what turn to make, whether it is driving on the highway, or what should be done at the next step of your life. This knowingness is a very important factor, being able to live from moment to moment without looking to the past or to the future, and living for this moment, now. Once one learns that little secret of not looking back or forward, he has a much happier and more productive life. He comes to learn to love all life and lets his fellow man just be. He gets lost in what he is doing and wonders where the time has gone when it's time to go home.

He does not interfere with another person's world or universe, nor does he allow another to interfere with his, because that world is for each individual alone. No person can tell you what is good or right for you but yourself.

There are no great promises made because this is not an easy path. It is the most disciplined path that exists in this world, but discipline is impressed upon the individual only by himself. He takes on only that which he wants for himself.

The emphasis is not upon the physical, although we can develop ourselves physically to a certain degree. Emphasis is placed upon the soul body, the finest vibration that is known. Science does not know its frequency and does not have the electronic equipment or oscillators or frequency generators that can tell you what the vibratory rate of the soul body is.

We travel on a sound current, much faster than the speed of light. It is precisely like a radio wave, issuing out of the center of that known as God and coming out to all of the world like a television or radio signal. It supports life as it is stepped down through the various worlds.

Light is knowledge. With knowledge of light alone, we can gain all life. One does not have to have the light because he can ride back to the Godhead on the sound current, once he learns to move beyond himself.

That awareness which you already have, you will not lose. You awaken to an even greater awareness. The mind is very limited. Once the individual learns to drop the complete body, including the mind, he goes beyond that known as the universal mind.

I was a loner as a child and young man, not getting in with groups or crowds, just in night clubs occasionally when I played music with the combo I had then. I sang in certain groups as a way to augment my living, and spent most of my time in the electronic field, designing magnetic components and other related components for the space industry and for various electronic instruments.

In working with physicists, scientists, doctors, PhD's and blue collar workers, I found there were a lot of people who had questions like myself. I wanted to know what was going to happen when I dropped this physical body, so this always kept me seeking. In my studies of the phyical life, about the sun and that magnetic force or those lines of flux that exist on this planet, as well as throughout the universe, which can be seen as light also, I tried to put the two, or twin aspects of God, the Light and Sound together, but I couldn't get anywhere. However, whether through deep contemplation, prayer or seeking through libraries, both philosophical and scientific, there was nothing I could find that would answer my questions and put out that fire within myself, until I met a spiritual traveler on the path. Once that took place, all the questions were answered in due time as I progressed.

I worked in various places and found that I had knowledge that others did not have. As a chief engineer without a degree, I replaced one who had a master's degree in math. He would work out a problem or design a component and it took him anywhere from a day to two days to do this, where I would look at the specifications, choose the metal and copper, or the number of turns and all the components that went into it, and put it together, and ninety times out of one hundred, I'd hit the right design very quickly, with just a few calculations.

Along with my knowledge of music from childhood where everything has a particular frequency, I worked out the mathematics elsewhere on the astral plane and on the mental plane. There are a number of ways one can help himself and not appear to be different from anyone else. I was questioned many times on where I got my answers because I did not keep exacting records. I wrote down certain notes or numbers, and I'd trust them. And the vice-president in charge of manufacturing for this firm took everything as I gave it.

All in all, this teaching has given me a set of values in my life I had never had before. My life changed when the masters entered my life, and I didn't question them. I have seen some of the masters throw rocks at each other. In the physical body, if someone's impressing his thoughts and ways upon you, you do not have to let him. He is interfering with your universe and world.

Your wildest and most far-reaching dreams are only a small part of what you are going to learn. You can break out of that clay shell and start to experience that bliss that exists within the other worlds. It is a question of survival.

Chapter 12

DYNAMICS OF LIFE

All life is a spiritual experience. The greatest principle of life, remarkable in its simplicity, is--Soul exists because God loves It. All life exists because it is God's Will that life exists, and this is the basic foundation of life, the whole of the philosophy of the teachings of the Masters and understanding.

The basic law of life can also be called the law of realization, for when one seeks for God, he cannot always find God, so one must seek God in a way that is NOT seeking God. Which can be done by opening one's inner self to IT and letting it direct one's life as IT desires. It is an inner awareness, or realization, that is gained through grace, for without soul there would be no life anywhere on Earth or in any of the universes of God.

In Letters To Gail, Vol. II, by Sri Paul Twitchell, he states on page 52: "Now one of the ways you can measure or yardstick a person's problems is: The Dynamics of Life, or what you might call the Visions of Life. They are Self, Sex, Group, Mankind, Life, which means the flowers, plants, minerals, animals, insects, fish, etc.; MEST, meaning matter, energy, space and time, or the Earth materials which are inorganic; World of spirit or forces, and the Supreme Being.

"The tensions, conflicts or introversions of an individual's life can be on one dynamic, or all. For example, one can be introverted on Self, meaning that he is completely aberrated on Self, talks about himself, puts all attention on Self, lives only for himself....These Dynamics are actually streams of spiritual forces playing across the life of the individual."

Every new spiritual experience, combined with the situations that arise in life, widens the perception of the individual and brings about a subtle transformation within that being. When under the spiritual guidance of the Mahanta, the Living Master, the individual's spiritual nature changes continually, not only with the conditions of that person's life but because it is a law of all life that one either progresses or degenerates.

For the initiate who abides with obedience to the Will of the Spirit, there should be no problem, when desirous of reaching that imperishable consciousness known as the Akshar state, in receiving it.

One of the great laws of the universe is to love one another, because when we love others our heart and consciousness are relaxed and our attention is taken off self. We relax when we forget ourselves for that is the natural and universally recognized result. A tense person is wrapped up in himself (self-conscious) or his immediate family. His feelings and thinking about what has happened to him in the past or will happen to him in the future or what other people are thinking of him keeps him "self-conscious."

Is it true, is it necessary, is it kind? One of the most inflexible laws that cannot be ignored if one wants to make headway on the upward path. The ways of the five passions lead to the lower pits of hell.

The five passions: Anger, Greed, Attachment, Lust

and Vanity, are discussed throughout many writings, and are gradually pried loose from the initiate who follows the disciplines and guidance of the Mahanta, the Living Master at the temple within.

Living a spiritual life does not mean that you spend a great length of time in worship, prayer, meditation, or contemplative exercise. When I am asked what the spiritual life amounts to, all I can tell anyone is that it is LIFE. It is living life to its fullest.

The initiates truly do not go around talking about the principles, they live them. But when asked by someone unfamiliar with the teachings, he will step forward with both feet, yet be cautious and take one step at a time while doing so, for one is unable to give the teaching to others. They must catch it.

Creation is finished within the lower worlds. This is fact whether one believes it or not. It is time for man to get beyond the lower worlds into the pure positive God worlds. We may take an item, a piece of music, a poem or a chair that we build and rearrange the material things to manifest them in some manner, and we call it a new creation. But it isn't really new for we have just rearranged matter or words. Yet what Paul Twitchell has written in his books and discourses, is that which you will not find anywhere else. You will find some of the statements of Jesus there, or Krishna, Mohammed, Socrates, or Plato, or any one of the past teachers, but none of them are here in this plane or field of activity.

Once a teacher leaves the physical world he no longer has a grasp or hold on those followers in the physical. He is unable to assist anyone here on Earth; even Jesus is unable to. Those who were initiated

189

under Paul Twitchell are still being guided by him through the lower worlds, but he will release them at a certain point in their unfoldment, or turn them over to the present master.

Whether one has had a second initiation, a third, fourth or fifth initiation, it does not mean that they have worked out all their karma yet. Some will work for a period of years in one particular initiation before they get to the next. No two people will have the same experience with their initiation. Some have inner initiations before they come to this path, but it is still necessary to have them in the physical realm as well.

And this happens after a two-year study of the discourses as a general rule. Some who are into drugs or mentally disturbed will be held off because the spirit flow can create a vortex bent on eliminating their problems and some would find the going rough.

Drugs and spirit do not mix and if one is into drugs, it is best not to continue with his studies until he is completely free of the habit. Should he want help to overcome the negative habit he will receive it but he must be sincere.

The individual who is gaining this spiritual freedom we keep reading about, needs several tools to assist himself above and beyond the mental worlds, beyond that part of us as human beings which is called mind.

If you understand the factor of non-resistance, then you can start reaching into some new vistas or experiences as we think of them. Each moment of our lives should be one experience after another, and there are valleys and peaks and, as the Chinese spoke of it, Yin and Yang, ups and downs. Yet one is able to learn how to use whatever portion of the cycle one is in, whether it is the down cycle or the up cycle.

If you feel someone else projecting his attitude, feelings, or thoughts upon you, don't resist it. Let it go on by and don't hang on to it. This is how one gains a greater height in the Far Country.

We are all on the same level physically. No one else knows where you are in your spiritual growth and development. The Spirit or the Holy Ghost, is the vehicle that supports all life. This is the vehicle that we work with. We express it through our actions, our words, our thoughts, and the less resistance you put up to other people, their thoughts and actions, the easier it will be on you. For no one here on Earth, and this includes the initiate, is holier than the next person, such as some religionists try to make one believe when they put themselves above their audience.

To better understand this, recall the last time you went to the gas company or the water or electric company to explain that their employee read your meter wrong, and the numbers were higher than they should be.

If you try to argue with the clerk or teller, there is no way you can shake them up because they have been trained in this factor of non-resistance. Regardless of who steps up to that counter to give them a bad time, there is no one who can, and we have to become the same way, just as the priest, pastor, rabbi or evangelist is.

You can look at the lives of any of the masters on the path or the saints in the scriptures of man, and you will find that each one of these were spiritually fairly well developed, and did not put up a barrier to the thoughts or the actions of another person that came at them, emotionally, physically, or what-have-you. They merely side-stepped it. Even though they stood in the same place physically, they let it go beyond themselves.

There comes a time when those who are seeking the God-conscious state must make a choice, and this choice is always up to the individual at each step. The first time one reads a book, hears a lecture or tape on this subject, he himself must choose to take the next step. If there is anyone pushing you, just ask him to please step out of your psychic space, because that world and that universe is yours. Yours to command, to direct, and guide as you want it, because no one else knows how you within yourself feel about certain situations, certain things, whether it is listening to someone give a talk or reading a book.

When some people try to push something they have on you, and they come on pretty strong about it, as some of the religious groups do at airports, or on streets and on TV, you are under obligation to them if you accept it.

This happens daily whether we are at work, at play or at the grocery store shopping. They want you to be under obligation. They don't just make it available to you, they aggressively push it upon you.

One who is developing himself spiritually and expanding his consciousness may not be aware of it initially. Later he comes into this knowingness, knowing how to make his next statement, take his next step and meet with those he wishes to talk with. Life is to be lived and it is active, not passive.

Some get caught up in phenomena like astrology, clairvoyance and mental telepathy, but in time they should move on into other pursuits, since all of these are but steps on the path. Many who are not interested in such things have already been through these stages in past lives and don't need them.

I don't ask anyone to look up to me. If you can't look up to that which is spirit, which can be seen as light as well as heard as sound, and which is the spiritual body, the Mahanta, then you do not have much respect for yourself.

A transition takes place when one master leaves this plane of action or steps aside and another steps in, and not very many of the followers know this. It is very subtle and there is really no change in that which is known as the Mahanta-consciousness.

There was a transition period when Peddar Zaskq (Paul Twitchell) took the Mantle. It resulted in a raising of consciousness for the world in general, and the time that he spent here, there was a drastic change from 1965 to the fall of 1971, not only for the followers of the teachings, but for the world in general.

Even though we do not work with the masses but work with the individual, there is still that responsibility the living master has for the rest of those who are seeking, regardless of what part of the world or universe they are in. This responsibility is far greater than that of the Pope.

There are a great number of people who in the past read everything they could get their hands on, heard every psychic, went to every medium, including having been in a half-dozen churches, and finally gave up and lived the way they felt they should live. What was right for them worked and they did not let others direct their way from day to day.

You as an individual should choose, set a goal, head towards it, and if an obstacle is placed in the way, make a visual snowball out of it and throw it into the spirit and do nothing about it, just find a way around it.

We can get out of the lower worlds without bcoming too extreme, going too far to the right or too far to the left. Making strides towards having a 360-degree viewpoint and when placed in a position to make a choice, knowing that the choice is right when it is made; whether it is done within yourself or in a point of view out here. But that choice that you make is only for you, not for others. Sometimes the head of a business or a family must make decisions for the benefit of the group, but it will usually work out.

While death and the after-life was discussed by Paul Twitchell, he mentions some interesting aspects of this shifting of consciousness indicating that when one dabbles in the psychic games, ignorance is no excuse.

In The Shariyat-Ki-Sugmad, it is stated:

"In the relationship that men have with one another, it is found that the astral and the mental have the greatest vitiative effect upon others. Those who stir up the astral waves and create disturbances among the human races suffer terribly without knowing what they did or how they did it. This is the danger of the psychic worker in this world. Be aware and do not have anything to do with them, for your ignorance will not be acknowledged nor be a reason for mercy when you face the Judge of the Dead. Your record here is what it is and your next assignment, unless you are under the protection of the Mahanta, will bring about more lives and further hardships, as one who violated the Laws of the Sugmad."

Perhaps the reason why so many fear death is due to the remembrance of having passed over the borders of life into the next plane countless times.

"No one ever questions the judgment." Paul Twitchell continues in The Far Country. "No comment is made, no oratory for the defense, no pretended righteous condemnation of the prosecution. The prisoner himself makes no complaint and asks no favors. He understands that he is to receive judgment, the Law of the Sugmad from the highest world to the lowest." This statment refers to one's inner and dream state being.

This sober, somber episode greets each of us upon death, prior to our meeting with the master. Then the scene changes, for Yama, the King of Death, will be bypassed by the Initiate who is taken past this entity by the Living Master, and taken to the place that he has earned. His family and friends will miss his physical presence, but joy will prevail because they know he has moved out of the confining state of consciousness in the physical realm of existence. Knowing that one is not "gone," but only dwelling in another state of consciousness and wearing another body, the initiate will find death no threat or fearsome encounter.

We are the product of our thoughts and as we think, these thoughts are manifested. So if you are looking for trouble, you are sure going to have it. When you are in trouble, it is sometimes difficult to put the trouble out of your mind, or to side-step it, but if it can be looked at from that 360-degree viewpoint, the lesson can be learned and will be of value. The next time that you are placed in that position, you will know how to handle it.

One question usually leads to another and when the spirit gets ahold of us, we have to hang on and ride over the rough spots, enjoying the smooth portions. We will find that we get into an area where we do not ask questions, we listen.

Spiritual unfoldment must be done slowly. If it is rapid, one could wind up in the hospital because the energy that can be given to the individual in a human body is only so much. And if the individual is not prepared for this energy, he will just run around like a little mouse with its tail caught in a trap. There is a constant negative kal force that is always available for all people. Some use it and worship the kal or negative force, but one learns how to use it as well as the positive force to their advantage.

Loving all life with a detached love is one of the steps necessary, yet you must use great discrimination in how you give out the love that is within the heart. And that counts physical love as well; you just cannot spread it around or give it to everybody.

Many are teaching the masses out there to love everyone. To love your neighbor is great, only as long as it is with a detached love. One finds out that the parent does not own the child, that each individual must live his life his own way when he/she comes of age.

We want the best for those who are young and growing and want to give them everything we didn't have ourselves. At least the understanding of what man calls heaven, what lies beyond that which we cannot see with the physical eyes. If we can do that, if we can bring our children into an area of understanding even before they get out of grade school, we will have a far different world in which to live.

We are not here to change the universe, politically, socially or in any other way. This is a warring universe and there are always countries at each other's throats. Maybe someday they will wake up and it's best to let them have their scrapes like a couple of kids.

There are many who will be coming into and following the teachings, because it is the only path today that can give the succor that the rest of the masses out there are seeking.

If someone tries to give you something, look twice at it, and make sure there are no strings attached. It is great to receive and to give. It is always greater to give, but it is the same as with giving a part of your heart in circumstances of love. You want to be very careful whom you give it to, because many times giving in this manner backfires.

Rather than giving love, give good will. That is far greater than saying: "Hey, brother, I love you."

One does not know what that person will do with the love that is given to him, but give of good will and you won't interfere with that other individual's state of conscience. Conscience is the word, not trying to changes his conscience in any form.

This substance that sustains all life is only the essence of God. We learn not to really ask anything of IT but are very humble to become a vehicle for IT. I speak of IT, not only of the essence of God, but of Sugmad itself. One gets into the stream of life and becomes active in handling his responsibilities. It gives the individual a freedom far greater than the wind that blows outside or that stirs the dust around and shifts the sands of time. This freedom is to be experienced by us as individuals through the expansion of consciousness, regardless of who the individual is.

These are very hectic times, yet very exciting times, an exciting era on this planet. Those who have the ability to shift their state of consciousness and allow themselves to reach above time, space and matter in the soul body, regardless of what is happening around them, can not only enjoy the bliss that is spoken of and the treasures of heaven that most of us are waiting for at the end of our lifetimes, but consciously utilize the heavenly worlds, the pure positive God worlds here and now.

There are ways in which we can expand another's consciousness without their even being aware of it--even that of a child or an animal.

A friend of mine had an animal that had suddenly become unfriendly, and wanted to bite and scratch the family and neighbor animals. When the animal went to the vet for some treatment, the owner spoke to the pet while it was asleep, and when it came out of the ether, it responded warmly like its own self again.

Another technique older than mankind has been used in other planes and dimensions. We too are subject to this same subjective subliminal control by others. We must be aware of this for it happens in the movies and on television, even though it has been outlawed.

It's subliminal and not readily noticeable to the naked eye but registers in the subconscious mind. It is a way that industry has found to control the masses, inserting a frame of what they wish the viewer to do or buy in the film and some are aware of this. Metaphysicians and psychiatrists sometimes use a form of hypnosis to reach the subconscious part of man. It is limited but many use it to control others.

You can handle situations by not remaining too long in one spot mentally, but by getting beyond the situation and into the next moment, not hanging onto what is past.

I do not have the time to answer all the letters I receive that involve physical and spiritual problems or situations. But once the individual has written, the situation is already in the hands of spirit if the writer would only let go of the situation and let spirit work with it. I've had many tell me that once they posted the letter, the burden was lifted. It will work if the attitude of the individual is receptive and he does not push for an answer he wants.

Spirit may not have the same solution in mind for that individual. By turning the situation over to the Inner Master and letting go, whether it is a health problem, or a physical or spiritual one, know that it is being handled to your best interest. It is trusting that nothing can work antagonistically toward you if your attitude is kept positive.

The spirit catches us. It touches us and it selects us as vehicles and it leads us to this path. It is up to us as individuals to either accept the responsibility of taking the next step, or deciding to stop here and wait until another time. Don't be rushed into anything, including this teaching, because it is not easy. I'm speaking from my own experience. It is difficult, it is rough, yet it is quite rewarding.

The treasures of heaven are now, and not tomorrow, nor when you reach the astral worlds nor the mental worlds. These are worlds of illusion and maya. The individual can prove to himself if he has the initiative to go to the temple within, which is only a starting point. This has much to offer the individual on how to heal one's self or others.

Do not form a group to try and sway legislators or Congress or other parties collectively. They work as individuals because of the reality and the experience that only you as individuals can experience yourselves.

Perhaps I can give it to some, and I have, and there will be others if there is a reason for doing so. But most have to work into it and develop it themselves, and as one is able and capable of handling more of that sound current known as spirit, more will be given.

We become positive channels for spirit. Some of us sense this in our physical bodies. For those who work on some of the higher realms, as they unfold and get the higher initiations, it is even more subtle as they go beyond the feeling point.

You know not only what you are going to be doing in the next successive moments, but if these moments are not working out, you can change the situation for yourself without letting others set up the conditions or relying upon another's thoughts.

The temple within is the area which you must be

acquainted with yourself first through self-realization, and then you must be bold and adventuresome and step beyond that into what is known as the Cosmic-Consciousness, similar to the Christ-Consciousness.

This soul consciousness far exceeds the Christ or Cosmic-Consciousness. Those who have experienced these consciousness states from past teachings, thought they were the ultimate when actually they are just the first rung on the ladder.

When one has gone through that dark void and been taken into the soul plane, it is up to the individual to go on his own. The master has turned loose of the individual and has taught him all that he can.

From there the individual makes the decision himself to go into the invisible worlds or endless worlds and on to the God-conscious plane to experience it while he is here. If this is your ultimate goal during this lifetime, you will never regret it. But remember, what comes with it is responsibility to yourself and to the Sugmad, no one else. To become a co-worker with God.

That is all the ancient teaching of the masters have to offer, a direct path to total awareness without holding back the secrets of God that are not known to mankind as a whole. Because once you learn them and know of them, you are not able to share them. There is no way you can.

That is why those who experience it come back here into this physical world, live their lives out and are humble servants of the Sugmad, happy to be ITs vehicle.

The only true wisdom I am able to give you is for you to learn to sing the HU, the easy way!

BOOKS BY DARWIN GROSS

Awakened Imagination

The Power of Awareness

The Atom

You Can't Turn Back

Available from SOS Publishing,
PO Box 68290
Oak Grove, Oregon 97268

For further information on
book, music & study program brochures,
please contact SOS Publishing.